Squeaky's Farm

Our Lives in Rural Spain

Squeaky's Farm
Our Lives in Rural Spain

Carolyn Parker

Illustrated by Bronwyn Holmes

DANCING MOON PRESS
NEWPORT, OREGON

Squeaky's Farm: *Our Lives in Rural Spain*
copyright © 2011 by Carolyn Parker
All rights reserved

Parker, Carolyn
Squeaky's Farm: Our Lives in Rural Spain
1. Title; 2. Cats; 3. Adventures of a cat in rural Spain; 4. Madroñera,
Spain; 5. Extremadura, Spain; 6.Farming in rural Spain.

ISBN-13: 978-1-892076-82-3
Library of Congress Control Number: 2010941265
Manufactured in the United States of America

"The Rule" reprint permission granted by David McReynolds
Cover and interior illustrations by Bronwyn Holmes
Cover design & production Jana Westhusing, StudioBlue West
Book design Carla Perry, Dancing Moon Press

DANCING MOON PRESS
P.O. Box 832, Newport, OR 97365. 541-574-7708
www.dancingmoonpress.com / info@dancingmoonpress.com

FIRST EDITION

Squeaky's Farm

Our Lives in Rural Spain

For Squeaky

You came to Scott and me from the streets of Seattle, abandoned, frightened, no traces of a family connection. We were to have you with us in our home only until you recovered from your spaying.

It was impossible to think of our lives without you after your recovery. You stayed, learned to love us, to feel safe again. You overcame unthinkable obstacles to move with us to a remote farm in Spain. Rest assured, brave old cat, we will never again ask you to make a long, cramped international airline flight in the pressurized pet section of a cargo hold.

We will always be grateful for the lessons you have shown us. The three of us have shared almost nine lives of adventure since meeting. Six years of farm life in Spain would never have been such a rich and poignant experience without you.

The Rule

There is a rule about cats: if you have only one cat, you become a cat. The universe is the cat and you, and the cat does not differentiate. If you have two cats, they relate primarily to each other. If you have three or more, I think you don't exist at all. The cats become a tribe unto themselves.

—David McReynolds

Introduction

Squeaky's Farm is the story of Squeaky, our now fifteen-year-old cat, a dearly loved, highly respected family member. After her harrowing early years on city streets, Squeaky chose to spend the rest of her life with us. She may have been re-thinking that commitment after we flew her to Spain's Extremadura region to live at Lagar La Señora, a dilapidated near-ruin of a stone house at the center of a rustic seventeen-acre farm.

In Extremadura, "lagar" can mean "farmhouse," "rustic farm," "place where olive trees and vineyards grow," or "building where wine-making equipment is located." It was all of that for us. Lagar La Señora is more than a century old, sparking memories of times gone by.

Our kind of farm. At the time we were there, life was still simple, even primitive. The closest *pueblo* (village) was Madroñera, about a mile down the hill from our new home, where we brought our tired, frightened cat in the spring of 1999. Squeaky faithfully rose to the occasion. Her feline sense of adventure prevailed, as did her choices from the heart when it came to sharing life with us in very unusual circumstances. We are grateful she didn't give up on us.

In retrospect, our transition with Squeaky happened at a time when Spain was rife with historical and political change. In the year 2000, Spain replaced their monetary system, the *peseta*, with the new European Union currency, the *euro*. What followed was a bubble from rapidly rising inflation, escalating real estate prices and an economic boom fueled by easy credit and high expectations for the new currency.

September 11, 2001. Member countries of the European Union, including Spain, reacted with sorrow and, initially, great compassion for the United States when they learned of the barbarous, calculated Al-Qaeda attack on New York City's World Trade Center, which took three thousand innocent lives.

On March 14, 2004, Al-Qaeda sympathizers struck Madrid, killing scores of victims during commuter train rush hour. The world and our European allies were again shown the harsh realities of open borders, lax immigration policies and the interdependence of world economies and stock markets. The Madrid attack was instrumental in the election landslide victory of Spain's political Left a few days later.

The Prince of Asturias, heir to the Spanish throne, announced his engagement to a commoner, breaking the age-old tradition of maintaining royal bloodlines. Even though his parents, King Juan Carlos and Queen Sofía, gave their blessing to the couple, the engagement spawned national debate for months. Love won. Prince Felipe and Spain's popular national television commentator, Letizia Ortíz Rocasolano, were married in May 2004.

In Spain's larger, modern cities, the number of animal rights activists substantially increased. Their first target was bullfighting, the centuries-old national passion, a death drama between man and the noble bull. The activists felt bullfighting was cruel to the *toros* (bulls), that it represented "old Spain," and that the practice should be eradicated.

The dynamic of traditional Spanish family life was changing. In large cities, it became the norm, not the exception, for families to have two income earners striving for upward mobility. Many of these couples had come from small pueblos where their parents still lived. Day care centers were created in the cities so that both parents could work outside the home, replacing the family tradition of live-in *abuelos* (grandparents).

The word *estrés* (stress) infused conversations as Spaniards embraced modern technology. Cell phones, computerized business systems, anything that enabled work to be done faster and faster became standard practice. Microwaved meals, deli foods, pizza, and fast food burgers displaced but, thankfully, did not destroy the excellent traditional cuisine of Spain.

Two-car families, traffic jams, air pollution, and hectic lifestyles in Spain's major cities became commonplace as was the case almost everywhere in the world as the New Millennium began.

We couldn't have picked a better place than Lagar

La Señora to get off the beaten path. Driven to reconnect to the land, to find real artisan products, and to gain the wisdom of local people still connected to traditional lifestyles, we eagerly anticipated living out the rest of our productive lives at Lagar La Señora. Having Squeaky with us was the icing on the cake. She intuitively knew how to enjoy the simple life.

Chapter 1

Squeaky's Checkered Past

No one knows what the first years of Squeaky's life were like. My friend Diane rescued Squeaky after seeing her wandering around her neighborhood. The cat was scrawny, hungry, flea-infested, not feral—but reluctant to trust strangers. She wore no ID collar. She was homeless, nameless.

Diane is a cat-lover supreme and soon coaxed "kitty" into her garage to feed her. The cat was leery and distant. Diane had adopted eight cats over the years, and felt her felines wouldn't accept another one. She posted Found Cat posters with a photo all through her neighborhood. No response, even after several weeks. No telling where Squeaky had traveled from or what her circumstance had been.

Diane and I spoke often about Squeaky's plight. Love of cats has always been a big part of our friendship. Diane knew our cat, Dishes, who had been with Scott and me from six weeks of age to nineteen years. Dishes had died one year earlier, after all our wonderful years together. Scott and I missed her terribly, yet we were like parents when their kids leave home: routines lighten up, priorities change and you begin to renew interests you enjoyed "pre-kids." Even so, little pangs of longing for the wonderfulness of cat companionship again crept into our hearts.

"No, Diane, don't ask me to do that," I protested when she suggested we adopt Squeaky. "But I'll go halfsies on getting her ready for adoption: vaccinations, bathing, spaying, placing ads for candidate parents." We agreed that Diane would take Squeaky in for spaying and that I'd care for her while she recovered. After that, we'd quickly find Squeaky a home.

I'll never forget it. Diane and I met halfway across Seattle in the parking lot of a natural foods cooperative one rainy morning. She had just picked up Squeaky from the vet. Squeaky was still sedated and fragile on a blanket in the basket Diane had prepared to keep her warm. Diane said the vet calculated that Squeaky was about two years old and might have had kittens at some point. I rushed to put the limp cat in my car and thanked Diane for all her efforts. "We'll get her rested and recovered, then find a good home for her," I said, trying to stay focused on the logical path to take.

I talked to Squeaky all the way to West Seattle. She was woozy, but I figured she could hear my voice. I told her she had been at the vet's office for a flea bath and an operation. Now we were going to my house to keep her safe. "You're going to have a nice, long rest. You need to be pampered for a while. When you feel better, we'll find a family to love you."

Diane had suggested that I choose one room in the house to be Squeaky's domain. I chose my office because we could keep the door closed. I placed a laundry basket on the floor, filled it with soft, clean blankets and pillows, and gently placed Squeaky into it. She was still wobbly and couldn't stand on her own. I petted her, told her everything would be all right, made sure she had food, water and a litter box nearby. I started to leave the room but glanced toward Squeaky once more. She was struggling to stand. "Give her time to adjust," I told myself. She's been living a homeless, frightened life. Now she's had surgery and is in a strange place. But my heart told me what she needed was gentle cuddling.

I lifted Squeaky ever-so-carefully and, stretching out on the floor with a towel over my chest, I placed her on top of me so she could feel a heartbeat. As I petted her, I tried to soothe her with my words. "Poor kitty, poor little lost soul. We'll find you a happy home."

She purred and lightly kneaded my chest like mother cats do in order to bond with their offspring. My heart melted as I held this frail, abandoned creature. Cat to human, we silently bonded. I put her back in the basket so she could sleep. Hours later, I heard a faint, squeaky meow and rushed in to see her. She was standing, shaking in her basket, looking pretty pathetic. I petted her as she sank back down into the blanket, still exhausted. "You need to rest, sweet little kitty."

The next day, Squeaky was strong enough to eat

and drink, use her litter box, and sniff around the room a little. By Day Three, I'd pass the closed door and see her little paw sliding under it, trying to find a way out. She was ready to meet the world again. I let her venture into the house, exploring, sniffing everywhere. Each day she gained strength and became more playful, seeming to feel safe and comfortable with us, no longer suspicious of humans.

It had not been my plan to adopt Squeaky. "No," I'd tell myself and Diane, "This is the time for Scott and me to be free of pet responsibilities. I can't waver on finding someone to adopt her." But my heart was saying what we all knew: Squeaky was home. Scott loved her determined spirit and gentle, playful nature, her exquisitely expressive face. She was a beautiful gray/brown longhaired tabby mix with sparkling topaz eyes, and we were smitten.

"Look, Carolyn," he announced one day as we half-heartedly hashed and re-hashed options for finding a suitable adoptive home for the cat. "Let's just keep her with us. She's already family."

It felt so right. She'd be "kitty" no more. We named

her "Squeaky" because, by then, we had fallen in love with her peculiar soft, halting meow.

After two years with us, and good vet care, Squeaky's skin was back to normal. No more fleas or flea dermatitis, although she couldn't bear to smell anything that reminded her of flea shampoo. She became a pretty, silky, well-mannered, playful, smart, sociable, mostly indoor/sometimes outdoor kitty. She loved us and her secure, comfortable environment. No more worries for this ex-street cat; life was good. The three of us were very happy together.

Then, on one of our many trips to Spain, Scott and I uncharacteristically cast our fate to the wind by purchasing a seventeen-acre farm with a dilapidated stone farmhouse in western Spain's Extremadura region. We decided to retire early, while we were still physically able to take care of 1000 grapevines, 500 olive trees, 40 fruit trees, and a few almond, walnut, and chestnut trees. Repairs could be done on the stacked stone, white-washed house that would provide enough amenities to live there permanently. We would enjoy excellent water from a deep well pumped by a generator into a cistern, indoor plumbing, and a large fireplace. A few tacky fluorescent light tubes charged by the generator, and sometimes by the little solar unit, were the only lights in the house. The existing solar panel and generator would be suitable for minimal energy consumption our first year there, with either more solar panels or a conversion to electricity later on if we wanted to do that.

Scott didn't speak Spanish very well, but I looked forward to the opportunity to refresh my Spanish language skills and figured I'd be semi-fluent in no time. We'd sell the Seattle house, most of our furniture, and catapult ourselves into a new, adventurous chapter in our lives.

On our return to Seattle, we were giddy with dreams and plans. Except for one big issue. Over and over we asked each other, What happens to Squeaky? Should we take her with us? Or, almost impossible to imagine, should we find a new home for her?

Trying to be objective, I said to Scott one evening, "A good mouser is probably what we'll need when we move to Spain. Squeaky is spoiled. She's an occasionally outdoor kitty used to attention and creature comforts inside. Special food, regular vet check-ups. You and I are just a meow away in case she needs us. I worry that the harsh trip and the strange new environment would be too much of an adjustment for her. Will she run away when we arrive at the farm?"

Before Scott could even answer me, I blurted out, "But I love her and want her to be with us. I can't just 'give' her to someone. She's been with us for more than two years. It would be abandonment."

I glanced at Squeaky, curled on her favorite swivel chair by the picture window. Just looking at her softened my heart. I knew she was only pretending to snooze. She was listening to us discuss her plight. Her ears pointed straight up.

"Oh, well," said Scott, too tired to get into this long discussion with me again. "Let's sleep on it."

The next morning we let Squeaky out for her ritual yard-sniffing as we continued discussing our plans for moving to Spain. Suddenly, we heard a gurgling meow at the front door followed by a big thunk. Was she sick? Injured? We hurried to open the door. There was Squeaky, triumphantly offering us the mouse she had hunted and killed! She had never done that before. We hadn't even realized there were mice around the property. She gazed steadily at us as if to say, *"So you need a mouser?"* Scott and I shared a knowing glance. We were flabbergasted but the message was loud and clear. We picked her up and held her close.

"Yes! Yes! We'll all go to Spain. Squeaky, you are such a smart kitty. You showed us you wanted to stay with us." No turning back now, we three would be inseparable.

Chapter 2

The Fur Flies

Our Spanish adventure was waiting to unfold as we left our secure life in the suburbs of Seattle, Washington. Two suitcases, two carry-ons, one large, taped, sturdy cardboard box, and a frightened cat in a kennel were our entire world. Scott and I wove our way through the serpentine line at British Airways International passenger check-in at SeaTac Airport, each of us guiding a luggage trolley through the narrow spaces, speaking calmly to Squeaky as we inched forward. "You're okay, Squeaky. Remember how we talked about the trip to Spain? You are going to be an international traveler."

Over and over we tried to alleviate her fear and calm ourselves by speaking quietly and matter-of-factly. She wasn't happy being thrust into her kennel at home and driven to this scary, noisy place. If she could just break out of the kennel, she might find a place to hide from all the feet pounding, incessant loudspeaker announcements, the rolling wheels of luggage, the beeping and honking of airport courtesy shuttle vehicles. She was trapped, cut off from familiar scents or land-marks. Only once in a while did she seem to realize it was us leaning down to the kennel door, talking to her. Her eyes were alert, trying to understand the sudden change around her. She pressed close to the back of the kennel, wanting to hide, fearing she couldn't rely on us anymore. Fight or flight was now her only hope and I could sense she was pondering the two alternatives. Nervously, I checked the latches on the kennel again.

"Good afternoon, passports and tickets please," chirped the airline flight attendant working at the check-in counter. After verifying our information on her computer she said, "Welcome, Mr. and Mrs. Parker and Squeaky. You'll be traveling to Madrid via London."

She quickly hoisted our luggage and boxed goods on the conveyor belt while we spoke to her check-in co-worker about our reason for going to Spain with our cat—a new life on a rustic farm was an adventure we couldn't imagine without her.

For some reason, the flight attendants' faces softened when they brought Squeaky's kennel onto the platform. We all peeked in, hoping to reassure her. Squeaky didn't want to be noticed. She huddled, silent and watchful, waiting for a chance to escape. Did they sense her fear and our insecurities about taking her on this journey?

After examining all of Squeaky's health records, confirming that we had booked a reservation for her in the pressurized animal cargo section, and that she was traveling in a properly configured kennel, one of the them told us, "We'll keep Squeaky here, under the counter, until it's time for the flight crew to board. Then we'll take her with us and make sure she is boarded in the animal section of the plane."

What a relief. Squeaky wouldn't have to wait in a cargo area in her kennel for hours until someone boarded her on, what we could only hope, was the right plane.

As they attached the flight information codes to her kennel, the women commented that I had already taped a laminated note on the top. On it, I provided our names and Squeaky's as passengers, our flight numbers, and emergency contacts if we were separated during the journey. Near the note, I had taped a small plastic zip-top bag with a little dry food and instructions for care and feeding during her legally-required transfer to an airport veterinary center between flights in London.

"She'll be fine, don't worry," the flight attendants said encouragingly.

We choked out, "See you soon, Squeaky," and walked away, hardly able to leave her.

From her perspective, we had taken her in a "cage" to an unfamiliar place, left her there unable to get away, and walked off. Her best friends, she must have felt, were abandoning her.

We had checked in hours early because we were traveling with a pet. On international flights, pets are not allowed to be in the cabin with you. They must travel in the cargo hold of the plane, in a pressurized area with temperature control, inside an airline-approved sturdy travel kennel. Sedation of pets is not permitted because they are unsupervised once boarded. Extra time is required at passenger check-in to review the animal's health records, flights, final destination, and emergency contacts. During passenger check-in, companion pets are usually transferred to a holding area, then transported to their section of the plane when the luggage is loaded. What a blessing that the flight attendants spared Squeaky the anxiety of being subjected to the clamor of a holding area, forced to wait there for hours.

It would be a long time before our plane left for London. We wandered around the airport shops like zombies, reviewing trip plans in our minds, trying to distract ourselves from the pitiful scene of Squeaky under the airline check-in counter.

"Scott, I have to see Squeaky one more time to make sure she's okay. I won't be long."

Quickly, I headed back to within visual range of the check-in counter. I had already passed through the airport security system so couldn't re-enter the area. But

15

I could see what was happening. The flight attendants were checking in the last batch of passengers for the flight. Squeaky was still in her kennel under the counter. She seemed to sense I was near because I saw her creep up to the wire door of the kennel. Then she saw me. Squeaky stared at me with terror in her eyes, her only greeting a sorrowful, heart-wrenching meow. I wanted to get closer so I could reassure her, but I couldn't risk breaching security. The flight attendants glanced knowingly at me, but continued checking in passengers.

I said, as loudly as I could, "Squeaky, you'll have to be a brave kitty. You'll be fine. We'll see you in Madrid."

I probably shouldn't have gone back to see her. Feeling like a villain, I turned and walked away from her once again, imagining that poor Squeaky was reliving the abandonment of her earliest years.

At long last, we boarded our flight for London. Scott and I were exhilarated, exhausted, and worried all at once. We embraced before we took our seats on the plane for that first and longest leg of the flight, happy to be just where we yearned to be. Silently, both of us wondered if we were about to run out of the good luck that had blessed us through twenty-one years of marriage. Mostly, we worried about Squeaky. All the way to Spain, I imagined her cowering in her kennel.

I whispered to her as if I were by her side. "Be brave on your journey, little friend. We have not forgotten you."

Squeaky would live in an anguished state, in limbo, for more than twenty-four hours, counting flight times, airport layovers, temporary quarantine in London, and airport Customs in Madrid. All alone in her kennel, no one to rescue her, no one to soothe her, no explanation for the sudden noises, no sense of location. No rest, no fresh water, food, or litter box. A dark room. Barking dogs in kennels nearby. She would slink to the back of the kennel, terrified by her imprisonment.

Where are you, Scott and Carolyn? Please don't leave me here!

******

Our flight arrived on time in London. We had been told that Squeaky would be transferred first to a holding facility for animals in transit to check her condition after the flight. She would receive food and water. Then a

17

shuttle van would deliver her to the connecting flight to Madrid and put her onboard. Leap of faith for me on all counts.

After a four-hour layover, Scott and I boarded our British Airways flight in London, destination Madrid. A mere two-hour flight on this last leg of our long airplane journey to Spain. We had been worried about Squeaky since leaving her with the flight attendants in Seattle. Did she get sick in her kennel? Did she die of fright because of the airplane engine noises? Did the British vets mistakenly put her in a six-month quarantine? On and on my mind raced, but I was trying so hard to be nonchalant. I didn't want my brooding about Squeaky to ruin Scott's anticipation of finally fulfilling our dream of a new life in Spain. As we walked to our seats, past two flight attendants, I recognized one of them from our Seattle flight check-in. At the same time, she said, "Are you the folks traveling from Seattle with a cat?"

"Yes," I murmured, my heart in my throat, afraid of what she might say next.

Her face beamed with good news and she calmed my apprehension. "I just saw her. She's on board this flight and she's fine. You'll be reunited with her in Madrid."

Precious words. Tears of relief streamed down my face. "You're very kind to let us know," I said, grateful for her concern. "Thank you for the good news."

Scott was as happy as I was, his endearing boyish grin reflecting our relief. "I told you she'd make it," he said.

Our spirits soared again. We'd all be together soon. I sank into my seat, feeling a huge weight lift from my shoulders. "Oh, Scott, it's finally going to happen." I reached for his hand, as was my custom during take-off and landing. "We're going to live our dream." I chuckled as I recalled my brother-in-law Bud's shock when I announced our plans to move to Spain and live on a run-down rustic farm in a house with no electricity.

"Is this the Carolyn Parker I know? The one whose idea of camping is to stay at a motel on the edge of the camp ground instead of sleeping in a tent? Now you're moving all the way to Spain to live like you're camping?"

"Yes," I admitted, laughing at my change of

perspective. "Who would have guessed? But at least I'll have a roof over my head!"

As I closed my eyes, hoping to snooze, my mind created pretty pictures of Squeaky playing in the vineyard as we worked near her. It was just as well that I couldn't imagine the bittersweet realities ahead of us.

The flight was much shorter than the time we spent in the Madrid airport after landing. First stop was at International Arrivals, where long lines of incoming airline passengers were routed single file to waiting Immigration officials. The officials unhurriedly ran computer checks for authenticity of documentation. Hundreds of people searched for their documents while the line moved along at a snail's pace. Scott and I just wanted to be reunited with Squeaky. As we approached the Immigration official who would screen us, Scott looked past the glass partition toward the baggage claim area. "There's Squeaky! She made it!" Beaming, he added, "Her kennel is going around and around on the luggage carousel. They must have taken her off the plane first."

I saw her, too. What a relief to see her, even from a

distance. Soon we'd be together. Passports, Residency Visas, police questions, animal health records, conversations with the Immigration officials about our planned life in Spain. Everything was in order. All the attention to detail before the trip paid off.

"Let's go rescue Squeaky!"

We hurried to the baggage area where suitcases were now appearing on the carousel conveyor belt. Ours arrived promptly and we arranged them on our luggage trolleys with our carry-on suitcases.

"Scott, where is Squeaky?" She had disappeared from view!

"They probably shuttled her off somewhere else because we weren't here fast enough."

"Where would they take her?" I asked, about to panic.

Some passengers near us were still waiting for their luggage to appear. One of them heard our conversation and said, "Oh, that's your cat? She was the first off the plane, I guess. She twirled around and around on the carousel in her kennel for about twenty minutes. Poor thing looked so frightened. We wondered why no one was here to pick her up."

"Immigration lines were really slow," I hurriedly explained, not wanting to take my eyes off the carousel in case Squeaky appeared. "We saw her from the window but couldn't get to her until we went through the check-point. I'm so worried! She's had such a long trip, all the way from Seattle. Now I don't know where she is."

"All the way from Seattle! What a brave cat!"

Suddenly, Scott spied the kennel on the carousel. "They must have taken her off for a while because no one picked her up, then put her back on because there were still passengers waiting for luggage."

I looked where he was pointing and saw her too! "Squeaky, Squeaky, we're right here."

I shouted her name again over the tremendous noise, unable to control my joy, not caring if I appeared like the nervous wreck I was. "Here we are, sweet kitty. We're coming." Finally, the kennel was near enough to pick it up. Some of the passengers applauded when we reached for it. Scott swooped her off the carousel onto our luggage trolley, setting her on top of our suitcases so we could see her face-to-face. She looked exhausted, frightened, dazed.

We tried to reassure her. "Squeaky, we're all together now. You're safe." She wobbled forward in the kennel, looking us right in the eyes, and greeted us with a very unhappy, trembling meow. She wanted out of the kennel but we couldn't give her the freedom she was due. It was too risky. She might get away from us and run. But at least we were with her now.

"Squeaky, I told you we'd see you in Spain!" My voice was breaking with the love I felt for this special cat who endured so much to join us in a new life.

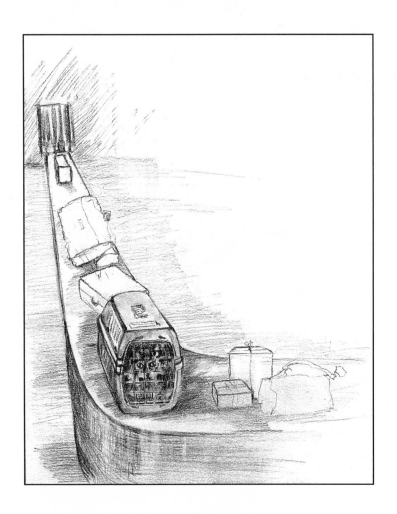

Chapter 3

Shelter From The Storm

"Hurry! Let's get Squeaky into the car first, out of the bad weather. Then we'll load the rest of our things," I suggested, as we exited the airline terminal in Madrid to pick up a rental car.

Hours of airline travel finally behind us, we were eager to complete our long journey home. Darkness, strong winds, and pouring rain were the only greeting for us as we navigated our baggage carts across terminal traffic to the uncovered rental car lot. Tired, hungry, cold, we focused solely on our immediate goal: getting the three of us safely to our farm.

Scott and I were on automatic now, unable to relax

and savor the moment. We moved as fast as our jet-lagged bodies permitted as we steadied Squeaky's kennel on the back seat of the car. Then we rushed to pack our luggage and boxes into the remaining space, and in the trunk. A quick check of the car's gauges and switches to make sure everything worked, and we zoomed south on the freeway.

"Squeaky, how's my sweet kitty?" I'd ask at intervals as we sped down the freeway to Extremadura. A weak meow would be her response. No doubt she was too exhausted to protest her circumstances. I hoped at least that she was comforted by being with us again. Three hours later, we were in rural Spain, close to our farm. Visibility was worse now as there were no city lights to guide us, nor stars, nor moonlight. And the rain had not let up.

Fortunately, Scott's inner directional radar hadn't short-circuited, and he remembered how to get to the farm from Madroñera, about a mile away. Driving the rented low-to-the-ground car presented a challenge as we bounced over the rocky, steep, winding old road traveled by wagons and burros for centuries. Finally,

Scott pulled the car up to the gate of our driveway. He jumped out into pelting rain, with only the headlights to illuminate the keyhole of the lock on the rusted flat metal gate. Cold hands, numb fingers, fumbling to open a half-broken lock. So patient. Thoroughly soaked.

Miraculously, the lock clicked open before Scott drowned! As he climbed back into the car, his clothes as damp as our spirits, I wished I had an irrepressible sense of humor so I could say one little thing to erase the gloom. Nothing came to mind. Such a long journey; no words left to speak. Even Squeaky didn't make a sound.

Scott drove cautiously down the driveway toward the house. The hard rain had caused flooding in low areas, making it difficult to see the driveway's edge even with headlights. At last, we reached the house! A new chapter of our lives was about to begin at Lagar La Señora. No fanfare. Great relief. Now we could all take shelter from the storm.

The house had two entrances, one covered by a small porch. "I'll go unlock the door while you get Squeaky out of the car," Scott said, already halfway there. I waited to get out of the car until I knew the door key worked. Magically, the key easily opened the locked door for Scott. I struggled to lift Squeaky, still silent in her kennel, out of the car. Being lifted into rain and wind sparked a weak meow.

Now what? She had no idea where she was, nor that it was the end of her travel.

"Squeaky, we are finally at our Spanish home! Let's get you inside so we can let you out of your kennel. You'll feel better soon."

As Scott turned on the solar-powered lights, we both breathed a sigh of relief. We had worried that the battery charge would be low because of recent overcast days. He closed all open doors and windows in the house to keep a frightened Squeaky from bolting through them when she was finally released from her kennel. We would all stay in one room that night, so that Squeaky could recover from the arduous journey and adjust to her new surroundings. Scott and I had seen the farm before, but Squeaky hadn't. She had no idea where she was. I grabbed the travel-sized litter box and plastic zip-top bag of clean litter I had packed in my carry-on suitcase for her, while Scott tried to read

Spanish directions for assembling and operating the two butane space heaters that were delivered to the house that day per our request.

Poor bedraggled Squeaky had been cramped in the kennel for more than twenty-four hours. Alone and afraid for most of the trip, she lived in the moment, as cats do. Survival is all that matters. Body temperature fluctuates, kennel-bound stiffness sets in, then dehydration begins. No escape from the confines of the kennel is possible. Luckily, the flights were uneventful. Plus, she was young and strong.

Squeaky had survived.

My long-yearned-for moment arrived as I opened the door of the kennel, speaking softly to her. "Squeaky, it's okay to come out. You're safe with us now. Welcome to your new home."

Squeaky probably wanted to scurry out of the kennel, but she was so weak she staggered out, almost collapsing. She let us pet her briefly, then limped to the litter box, looking greatly relieved to have a proper place again. It must have seemed like a little piece of heaven after a long trip through hell. The towel in her kennel smelled of urine. She had sat on a wet, stinky towel for a long time, unable to move somewhere else. Agony for a cat. They like to be clean.

A bowl for water and food, plus a little can of soft cat food and a zip-top baggie full of hard food were all swiftly taken from my suitcase. I knew Squeaky was hungry and probably a little dehydrated. I quickly filled the bowls with food and water. At last, she would get some nourishment.

"Squeaky, come over here. Look what a nice treat you have!" I cajoled.

Scott and I were so exhausted it would have been comforting to have someone take care of us at this moment. But Squeaky was our priority. She needed our love and reassurance. She choked down a few bites of food, lapped up a little water, but was too nervous to eat or drink much. Sniff, sniff, sniff. Slinking suspiciously across the floor. No familiar sights or scents except for Scott and me.

Where am I? Are there other animals here? Am I in danger, again?

I used a wet cloth to clean her, then quickly

brushed her matted hair. She was nervous and weak from the trip. So were Scott and I. It was very cold in the drafty room that would be our "bedroom" for the next few days until we could organize things well enough to make a more habitable place in the other side of the house. Rain still poured outside. At least the new roof, just completed that day, didn't leak. I made a mental note to tell Bud we arrived mere hours after the roof was finished, allowing me to "camp" with a roof over my head!

Scott got the heaters going and the cold, stone walls and bare floors of the room began to warm. We had purchased a bed previous to this trip and requested that it be delivered to the house. Thankfully, it arrived with the space heaters.

The last "luxury items" I took from the big suitcase were a set of sheets, two small pillows and, best of all, a down comforter! Real goose down, squished up like a mat in the suitcase.

"Now aren't you glad I decided to stuff that comforter in my suitcase?" I asked Scott, feeling very proud of myself.

It seemed silly when we were packing in Seattle to consider lugging a down comforter in my suitcase, but I had anticipated our arrival into cold circumstances and insisted that we bring it along. I hurried to get the sheets and comforter over the damp mattress so we could collapse into bed. We turned off the space heaters and the lights. By now, it was almost three o'clock in the morning, Spanish time.

Never more weary, Scott and I crawled into bed, pulling the comforter close around us trying to create some warmth. Almost instantly, the goose down kicked in as Scott's healthy body heat started to warm us up. In what seemed like just a few seconds, Squeaky joined us, as we hoped she would, purring contentedly, crawling all the way under the covers. After so much trauma, she needed to be with us. We petted her as she twirled around and around between us, seeking just the right spot for a long-awaited nap. At last, she could enjoy the pleasure of a comfortable place to sleep. Soon, she lay snuggled between her two "personal heaters" with her back feet on Scott's stomach, her head propped on my chest.

Scott pulled the comforter closer around us and

mumbled, "Squeaky, you're The Best. What a great kitty! But leave us some space, too."

I couldn't go to sleep without letting her know how proud we were of her. I whispered, "Squeaky, you are a brave cat. You must have been really scared. I'm sorry for all you had to go through. Did you remember we told you we'd see you soon? You won't have to get back on a plane for a long time. We'll have a great adventure here with our All-The-Way-From-Seattle kitty."

I stroked her soft fur, soothed by her purring, as she kneaded my arm with her paws. Three hearts, three kindred spirits, finally reunited after a difficult journey. Comforted by each other's presence, we quickly dropped off to sleep. All three of us together again. Safe, weary, and relieved to have survived the trip. *Familia* (Family).

After three or four days in this room, Squeaky would see the rest of the house and then, seventeen acres of farmland. So many discoveries awaited her. Her life, and ours, would be forever changed.

Chapter 4

A New Leash On Life

Sure enough, after a few days confined in one room, Squeaky was driving us crazy to get outside. Before we left Seattle, I had made a new ID collar tag for Squeaky to wear at the farm. "Squeaky, let's put your new necklace on you." I always called her collar a necklace. She's a girl kitty, after all. We added a harness and a leash, and for the first time since leaving Seattle, Squeaky stepped out into fresh air, her feet touching the warm, spongy earth of early spring in Extremadura.

We walked through the farm with our harnessed kitty to familiarize her with the territory. Had she expected to walk outside and find our Seattle yard? She was nervous being restricted by the leash because she couldn't run or fight if suddenly surprised. I think after a while, though, she figured out we were there to protect her from any danger. Eventually, she stopped fighting the leash and began leading us around as she sniffed her way through acres of huge olive trees, fruit trees, and hundred-year-old bush-pruned grapevines that looked like small trees. We lifted her onto one of the stacked stone walls that bordered and crisscrossed the property, where she could get a better view of her surroundings. The stone walls would become her favorite place for observation.

Back on the ground, she delighted in sniffing everything around her. Squeaky was finding her own way in this new world. Scents of fox, wild boar, sheep, geckos, snakes, mice, voles, fearsome feral cats, birds, and insects penetrated her senses. We strolled along at her pace, enjoying Squeaky's unique perspective. She showed us small, secluded spots we hadn't noticed when just the two of us saw the farm for the first time.

After several weeks of leash-walking through the property, Squeaky became so impatient with the process that we could no longer restrict her natural instinct to move at her own pace and explore her new world. Rationally I could accept what we needed to do, but my sense of responsibility for her safety created more question marks than reassurances at the moment when we were about to unleash her. Squeaky squirmed in anticipation, sensing freedom at last. At that moment I realized how unconditionally bonded I felt to this special creature. Perhaps it was like walking your child to board the bus for their first day of school. I pleaded for reassurance from Scott. "What if something bad happens to her or she gets lost?"

He just rolled his eyes and said, "Stop worrying so much! She's bonded with us, she'll run around a little, but still come back."

How in the world could he be sure of that?

"Okay, you're right," I conceded. "After all, we can't keep her on a leash forever!" I quickly unleashed her, silently saying a little prayer that she would have a happy romp and return to us.

Not wanting to place all my eggs in one basket, however, I had an insurance plan for her certain return to the house. I would use this for several weeks until her return became a natural part of her indoor/outdoor pattern. I made certain that when she went outside exploring without us that she was hungry. To encourage her to return to the house, I walked around outside shaking her bag of hard food, but didn't call her. She would hear the sound and return triumphantly from her field adventures to eat.

Squeaky was a very fast learner, so this little insurance policy wasn't effective for more than a few weeks. But by that time she had attuned herself very well to her new environment. Somehow, during her first month there, she instinctively evaluated stone walls and thickets as safe or not. Sheep grazing on our property were to be avoided or she would be squished underfoot. The shepherd's dog was a formidable, no-nonsense mastiff, so Squeaky would entertain herself elsewhere on the farm when he was guarding the sheep. Steller's jays and magpies were no fun to hunt or chase because they swooped down in large groups, pecking at the new feline stalker in order to drive her from their territory.

Squeaky's instinctive feline survival skills were

sharpened in no time as she noticed buzzards circling over sick or dead animals on nearby farms. She chose a safe place to watch hawks, eagles, and other native birds of prey as they competed with her for small mammals. Some of them were large enough to carry her off, too, if they were so inclined. She figured out mice were nesting in the stone walls, caught one, and proudly brought it to us.

Remember, you said you wanted a mouser.

She picked out her favorite observation points from lowest to highest: perch safely on the low stone wall in front of the house to get a quick one-hundred-eighty-degree look at that side of the farm. Go to the top of a hill for a better perspective.

Is there a fox walking across the farm again today?

Make a plan. Hunt for mice and geckos? Roam the fields to mark the territory as hers? Snooze under the shade of a grapevine? Take a dirt bath? Which olive tree trunk will make the best scratching post today?

Daily adventures on the farm for Squeaky weren't always satisfying but they certainly were continual learning experiences. Her first mishap nearly scared us to death. A beautiful late evening spring sunset framed the drama as Squeaky came running toward the house. I saw her from a window and quickly opened the door. "Squeaky, what's wrong? You sure are in a hurry." She rushed past me, moving erratically across the floor. "Good grief! Come here, poor Squeaky." She ran away from me, making frantic loops around and around the kitchen, stopping sporadically to lick her paws, her body, her face. Then she'd hide under a table, anxiously biting at herself. She looked terrified and seemed to be in pain.

"Dear Lord, what has happened to this animal?" I wondered if the previous owners had left some poison or pesticides in the fields. When we moved there, we discarded all suspicious-looking powders and liquids we found outside, but we knew that in many places things might have been tucked away, out of sight. Perhaps she had walked through something, then licked her paws. I kept trying to talk to Squeaky, to get her to come to me. She wouldn't. I had to crawl toward her and drag her out from under a counter. She struggled to get away but I held on tight. "Squeaky, let me look at you. Please, I want to help." I gently touched her face and stroked her body. She writhed to escape, unable to stand my touch. Had she been stung by an insect? The fields were full of ants, early-hatching yellow jackets, bees, wasps, as well as the dreaded poisonous scorpions that lodged in stone walls.

I saw no swollen areas so concluded she hadn't been stung. No cuts or broken bones. If she had been poisoned I imagined she would be vomiting or going into convulsions. Scott and I took her to a bedroom and closed the door so we could keep her in one place and monitor her. In the States, we would have called our vet, and even after regular office hours as this incident was, we could have gotten treatment for her. Just a few weeks before, we had taken Squeaky to the only local vet for her first check-up since arriving in Spain. No use calling him; after-hours service wasn't offered.

Scott and I were distraught as we watched Squeaky's misery unfold. She continued to dart around the room, still suffering. Her tongue stuck out of her mouth, a bright purple.

"This must be some kind of allergic reaction," Scott

41

said. "Carolyn, are there any plants she might have nibbled that would cause this reaction?"

I couldn't think of any at first. Then I remembered the huge patch of green stinging nettles near the stone wall in front of the house, the wall that was Squeaky's favorite perch. She may not have tried to eat the nettles, but could have jumped right into them while chasing a mouse. I had been stung by the nettles many times as I collected them to make nettle tea. Yet I hadn't anticipated that she might get near them. Maybe we had unraveled the mystery of Squeaky's dilemma.

"Well, the only thing I can think of that might help her is a homeopathic remedy for cats I brought with us from Seattle. It's used for calming itchiness and nervous scratching from fleas. She doesn't have fleas, so I've not given it to her yet, but maybe something in the remedy will help."

I went to find the tincture and quickly reviewed the instructions. Scott held Squeaky tightly so I could open her mouth with one hand and administer the drops with the other. We put her down and she dashed off, now in fight or flight mode. Our hearts sank. Had we made her condition worse?

"It probably takes a while for it to be absorbed into her system," Scott said hopefully. "Let's give it a few minutes."

Sure enough, in five minutes, Squeaky stopped twirling and biting herself. She still licked her paws and body, but seemed to calm down just a tad. I gave her another dose about twenty minutes later. That seemed to help a lot more. Her tongue regained its normal coloration; she sat quietly, still panting slightly. We could hold her and pet her now.

"Oh, dear little friend, we were so worried about you. It was horrible to know you were suffering and not be able to help you right away." I was relieved that everything worked out in Squeaky's favor this time, but felt guilty that our search for a simpler life meant veterinary care wasn't as accessible as we had anticipated, nor as modern.

Squeaky rewarded us with purrs and paw-to-hand touches. All was forgiven. Friends again. By now it was way past bedtime. We were all worn out by this adventure. I gave her one more little dose of tincture, hoping that by morning she would be fine. She was. Neither Scott nor I slept all night, getting up constantly to check on her. Next day we took her to the vet, just to make sure our analysis was correct.

"Oh, yes," he said. "It probably was the nettles. It happens a lot to animals this time of year. If it happens again, go to a pharmacy and ask for antihistamines for a cat."

That crisis survived, we all began to relax into our new life again, savoring the pleasure of our daily experiences together. Squeaky's enthusiasm for exploring her new Kitty Kingdom was undiminished. She especially liked being outside with us when we were doing our chores. Curiously, she seemed to make no real distinction between being "outside" with us or "inside" with us. Maybe the world really is just one big room to a cat, with a few partitions here and there.

The only inside/outside mystery Squeaky faced was the layout of our house. The structure had two distinct sections with separate entrances. The side entrance by the covered porch led to the fireplace room and then to our kitchen. The front entrance led to a little alcove, a small bedroom, and up a wooden stairway to a "living room," another bedroom, and a bathroom. In order to get from the bedroom upstairs to the kitchen it was necessary to go out the front door, around the corner to the covered porch and enter the side door. It wasn't possible to go through the house from one side to the other. Scott and I often left the side where Squeaky might be napping and went to the other side. Of course, she couldn't figure out how to get to us, because she couldn't open the doors! This obstacle kept her from coming and going at will, especially when we forgot to go back for her.

We decided to re-build the old *bodega* (wine making and storage room) that had collapsed. That task would also give us a way to unite the two parts of the house. We'd ask the carpenters to build two interior doors in the *bodega*. One would go into the downstairs bedroom, which would create access to the upstairs. The other would provide entry from the *bodega* into the fireplace room and kitchen. That solved numerous problems for us. For one thing, we wouldn't have to go out in the rain to get to the other side of the house. But Squeaky still wouldn't benefit unless we were always around to open a door for her. "Let's ask the carpenters to make two cat doors for her. That should be simple enough."

Most carpenters in rural areas of Spain were unfamiliar with making a door for a cat within an existing door. "Who would want a cat in the house anyway?" they asked.

"We would. It's not unusual in our country."

"Just leave the window open at night," they replied, sounding a little impatient.

"You know we can't do that; we had you put screens on all the windows! You have to make two cat doors." I pressed on to make my point. "There's no way to get from one side of the house to the other. It drives Squeaky crazy because she can hear our voices but can't find us."

Our friendly carpenters were amazed that a cat's frustration would matter at all.

"Just leave her outside all the time then."

"Not a possibility."

"Goodness," I thought to myself. "Their attitude is awfully similar to how folks in rural Virginia felt about cats when I was growing up."

I convinced them the cat doors were essential. But when they delivered the two big doors with the cat doors installed, the openings were big enough for only a rat to get through. Not a ten-pound cat.

"*Madre mía* (good grief), it will never work!" I challenged. "How could you make the doors so small? You've seen our cat."

They insisted she could squeeze through them somehow. Time for a visual. I grabbed an unwilling Squeaky, who, by the way, had never used a cat door in her life. I tried to push her headfirst through the little opening in the cat door so they could see that it was too small. She struggled to get away from me. The carpenters started laughing.

Stop humiliating me!

Squeaky raced out of the house as soon as I let go.

"*Gorda, muy gorda* (fat, very fat)," was the chorus.

Then I realized two things: the carpenters had never really noticed Squeaky when they worked there, because she was a… cat. A non-entity. Cats all look the same. And that, if by chance they noticed a cat, they were used to seeing feral cats. Skinny, scrawny, boney, diseased cats.

I insisted they make the openings larger. They agreed, begrudgingly, but we had to wait several weeks for them to return with the improved cat doors. The carpenters did a great job the second time. We used Squeaky again to demonstrate.

"If she can't get through this big door, she has to go on a diet," they joked.

She didn't take to being thrust through a hole with a hinged flap, but she made it through, easily.

"See," bragged the carpenters, "we knew exactly what to do."

Each time we saw them after that day, they asked if she was still using the cat doors. Oh, yes, she used the cat doors. Our training process was lengthy but Squeaky finally overcame her suspicions and loved the independence gained from this modern convenience.

Scott and I grinned each time we watched Squeaky charge gleefully through those doors. She had a built-in security system, though. If she sensed a person on the other side of the door, or if there was a strange noise, she'd poke her head just far enough through the cat door to check whether her cross-over would be a safe one before going through.

I don't like surprises.

Chapter 5

"Mama" Returns To Lagar La Señora

Squeaky's happy adjustment to *campo* (country) life crumbled one day when she encountered "Mama" and her feral offspring in the fields. "Mama," our name for this unspayed female cat constantly in heat or birthing weak offspring, had belonged to the previous owners of the farm. When we purchased the property, we requested that they be sure to take Mama with them to their new farm up the road. We said we were going to bring Squeaky all the way from Seattle, and didn't want a cat on the farm who would resent Squeaky's presence. They reluctantly agreed and took Mama with them. But she kept returning to Lagar La Señora. Mama loved the farm and was sure it belonged to her! Mama was a smart animal, able to survive in the feral cat world, yet at ease with people. She had been treated quite kindly by the young daughters of the former owners, more kindly than was customary in remote rural Spain.

Generally, cats were kept around only as mousers. They were rarely fed, and never spayed or neutered. They were not given names, nor particularly noticed. Their fate was to roam the *campo*, fighting for food, shelter and mates. They remained proud and independent regardless of their treatment by humans or predator animals and birds. Weak kittens and old or sickly cats were the most vulnerable, snatched by birds of prey, stronger dominant cats, or killed by humans who didn't believe in spaying or neutering cats but disliked having too many around.

Mama's face was testimony to her harsh life. One lower eyelid was red, slit, and filled with pus. We were told she had probably been grabbed for a meal by a fox or other predator, escaping with her life, but left with a mangled eyelid. The owners made a meager attempt to treat the eye, to no avail. Then they just figured it would get better or she would die. Simple. Just a cat, after all.

Scott and I liked Mama. She was a feisty old cat with a big ego. Very much an extrovert, she thought she was adorable. But *campo* life taught her that to stay alive you must be dominant and aggressive if you want food and a place to sleep. Go after the weakest link first. In our case, the weakest link was Squeaky.

Mama was on alert. Her chosen domain had been invaded by a city kitty unfamiliar with farm life and survival skills. It would be easy to oust Squeaky from the farm. Scare her, corner her, hurt her, watch her run away. Tried and true combat tactics in Mama's world.

I foolishly wanted the two cats to be friends and tried to incorporate Mama into our daily life when Squeaky was near. My acceptance made Mama feel superior—not the result I had in mind. Things came to a head one night on our front porch as Mama sat on my lap and Squeaky approached. Squeaky was leery of Mama but wanted to share my lap.

If Carolyn likes her, then I guess we can be friends.

Mama hissed and swatted. Squeaky cringed and withdrew instead of retaliating. In that moment, Mama dominated and Squeaky became the outcast. Squeaky looked at me as she retreated.

How could you do this to me?

I felt like I had driven a knife through her heart.

After that incident, Mama took every opportunity to intimidate Squeaky when we were outside. Squeaky's only sanctuary was inside the house, with us. Mama wasn't allowed there. But outside, Mama picked on her. Mama astutely observed, then sabotaged many of Squeaky's simple pleasures. Squeaky loved to walk down the driveway with me, stopping to roll in the dirt, to be petted and sweet-talked. Mama would run up, swat at Squeaky, then try to get me to pet her. I'd scold Mama, but Squeaky would leave.

It used to be fun to go for walks with Carolyn.

I knew Squeaky was confused. Her eyes looked sad so often, I wondered if she felt I didn't love her anymore. That was so far from the truth. I was heartbroken, too, that Mama was encroaching on our special friendship and I didn't want the tension to escalate into full-blown cat fights. I took the middle road, trying to be nice to both of them. The problem was, Squeaky had a fair sense of companionship, but Mama didn't.

Sometimes I'd find a long twig with leaves so I could play "chase and pounce" with Squeaky outside near the willow tree. Squeaky loved that game. We'd run around, me laughing, Squeaky practicing her feline crouch and pounce tactics. Until Mama decided to swat Squeaky out of the playground. Squeaky would hiss back once in a while, but Mama wasn't fazed.

Mama was comfortable with her self-proclaimed role as *Reina de la Finca* (Queen of the Farm). Worse yet, her numerous illegitimate, "gangsta" feral offspring roamed the farm, no longer afraid to approach the house. Mama had reinforcement for her efforts to banish Squeaky.

Chapter 6

Mama And The Gangstas

Squeaky sat alone on the hill near a stone wall just at the far border of our property, having been intimidated away from her favorite spot in front of the house by an increasingly dominant Mama and her brood of feral cats.

Squeaky waited, her long gray/brown hair providing the perfect camouflage with the slate-colored stacked stone wall behind her. Probably watching me work. Silently assessing the situation. Ears upright to hear any threatening sounds. Body crouched low in the dust under the shade of a Holm oak tree on this hot afternoon. Mama was near me in front of the house, having chased Squeaky away earlier. By then, it was easier for Squeaky to avoid confrontation than to resist Mama's relentless mission to run her off the farm.

When Mama wandered off to the far side of the house to take a nap, I seized the moment to look for Squeaky. I knew her spirit was wounded and feared she would run away if I didn't create some sort of truce between her and Mama. Casting an uneasy look over the farm, I saw no trace of Squeaky. My heart ached as I imagined her lost, alone, fearful. Slowly I walked up a hill, hoping to gaze over the farm and catch a glimpse of her. Quietly, so as not to alert Mama, I called, "Squeaky, Squeaky, where are you? Are you here? Please come to me. It's okay now." No response.

I felt drained, dejected. So many priorities to deal with on our farm as we navigated the extensive learning curve of our adopted lifestyle. Major learning curves to get us through the complicated bureaucratic process of obtaining Spanish driver's licenses; communicating with construction workers in the local *castúo* dialect, not the proper *castellaño* Spanish I had learned in school; learning to fuel and maintain the generator that provided electricity; and trying to find reliable workers to occasionally help with farm chores. We'd make mistakes, then try to correct them. But moving to rural Spain had been our choice. We feared Squeaky felt her only choice was to stay with us or run away.

As I climbed higher over rocks and through the parched olive grove, I fretted over the consequences of having brought her with us. What kind of life had we selfishly imposed on this innocent animal? Had she wondered why we didn't chase Mama away? Had Squeaky jumped the fence and disappeared forever, to be preyed upon by feral cats, foxes, shepherds' dogs? Had she given up on us? Tears filled my eyes as I realized how much uncertainty and upheaval we had inflicted on this gentle cat due to our decision to move to the farm.

Suddenly, I caught a blurred glimpse, a faint shadow, way up at the top of the hill. I cautiously approached, not sure if it was Squeaky or just wishful imagination. Then I saw her eyes reflected by the light! Partially hidden in the dry, prickly weeds, Squeaky was anxiously studying me. I quietly spoke her name, fearing she would run. She might think Mama was with me. "Squeaky, it's okay, I'm here alone."

She didn't move, although she made eye contact with me. I approached and she seemed ready to run, but didn't. I sat down near her, not too close, so as not to frighten her away. I wondered if she could hear my heart beating, as I could. There we were, perched almost together on a high hill looking toward the house. If she chose to run, it might be the last time I would see her. I had to speak to her from my heart.

"Squeaky, thank you for staying. Thank you for not jumping over that fence. I love you so much. I'm sorry to have made you suffer because I was kind to Mama and her mean family."

I waited, afraid to move. At last, a barely audible purr. She looked right at me with those sad, soulful eyes and seemed to make a decision. In an act of emotional surrender and trust, Squeaky rolled over and exposed her tummy for me to rub! My heart filled with gratitude and relief. She forgave me. She didn't run away! I petted her, thrilled to feel the silkiness of her tummy fur, comforted by her purring. Peacefulness prevailed as we sat there, re-bonded, on that hot summer afternoon. I picked her up and held her on my lap, reassuring her that we were forever friends, that I would always try to find her and protect her. I stroked her beautiful, expressive face and vowed to her that we would not let Mama ruin our lives on the farm.

"Squeaky, we are family. We must stay together."

******

Scott and I unwittingly aided and abetted the gangstas by providing food and water for them outside. We always fed Squeaky inside, but felt that maybe the gangstas wouldn't be so antagonistic toward Squeaky if they were well fed. Wrong in a big way. It made them more territorial. They wanted to be allowed in the house, Squeaky's only remaining safe spot. They found a way to get into a second story window, the only one we hadn't yet screened, and made their way to the master bedroom, found the bed, and claimed it. I just happened to walk upstairs and found them—four young feral cats lounging in the bed with Mama. I chased them down the stairs and out the front door, slamming closed the wooden shutter of the bedroom window so they couldn't sneak back in. I decided to leave it closed no matter how hot it might get. Squeaky would be the only feline to have the luxury of lying on our bed!

Gangsta Revenge: One dark night, the gangstas ambushed Squeaky. We heard her scream, a different kind of scream than the usual "get out of my way" or easily identifiable mating sounds. Chilling, vulnerable screams. I rushed out to find her, calling her name loudly. The gangstas fled as Squeaky came running to the door, frantic to get inside. I ran after her to pick her up. She was covered in poop. She had been pooping when those vicious feral cats attacked her.

Unintentionally, I traumatized Squeaky even more by grabbing her and trying to clean her off. I didn't want her to run into the house and spread mess everywhere. Horrible of me to think about that instead of her plight. I slung her under my arm so she wouldn't escape, which caused her to squirm even more to free herself. In crisis mode and not thinking clearly, I grabbed a bucket with my free hand, filled it with water, and tried to dip her into it to clean her off enough to assess damages. Squeaky was frantic, struggling to get away from me. She wanted only the safety of the house. I managed to wipe off most of the poop, saw no damaging wounds, and let her run inside.

Violated first by her feline enemies, then by my rough handling, Squeaky hid under a bed. I left her there for a while to calm down, while I washed myself off and changed out of my smelly clothes. Then, I tried to soothe her, sitting on the floor near the bed, apologizing for being so rough. She was hurt that I had been impervious to her need to flee. When she finally came out from under the bed, she reluctantly let me pet her, those usually-bright eyes dulled by confusion and betrayal. I gave her a head-to-tail check to make sure she hadn't been wounded in the fracas. Fortunately, I found no blood or telltale wounds.

"Squeaky, it was dark and I couldn't get to you fast enough to rescue you. You were smart to run to the house. I'm sorry about overreacting and scaring you even more. It's been unfair to you that the gangstas can come and go as they please. Please forgive me. I'll make it better." No purrs. Did she understand? I vowed again to make the Lagar a safe place for her. Scott and I were heartbroken. We hadn't anticipated feral cats would be around to make her adjustment to farm life so risky. We would have to stop feeding the feral cats, stop hoping they would accept her. We couldn't let them chase Squeaky away or harm her.

Mama's gangstas couldn't eke out a living at the farm after that. No more sympathy, no more attempts to "socialize" them. Squeaky had traveled with us all the way from Seattle, and she was our priority. The gang of feral male and female cats would go back to hunting for mice, rats, birds; to eating garbage left by weekend visitors at nearby farms; to murderous male fights for dominance in a tough existence. Female cats in that atmosphere are really breeders. They bear one litter of kittens after another, weaker and wilder each generation, fathered by stray males, from inside or outside the female's family. No catch/neuter/return programs existed. In the *campo*, the weakest die.

Soon, the gangstas were gone and Mama was the lone survivor. We decided to have Mama spayed so she would stop attracting roaming male cats to the farm whenever she was in heat, and cease birthing litters of weak kittens. She was pregnant too often to stay healthy. Maybe now there would be a reduction in feral cat births and the farm would be safer for Squeaky and Mama.

The trip to the vet was Mama's first experience in a kennel. She wasn't happy, to say the least. I'm not sure she had ever been in a car. She threw up in the kennel due to motion sickness.

When we arrived at the vet's office, Scott and I had to get Mama out of the kennel and wipe her off with the soiled kennel towel because the vet thought Mama was too wild for him to handle. While we restrained Mama, the vet quickly injected anesthesia, then began haphazardly wiping off the stainless steel operating table. Next, he thumbed through his vet schoolbook, double-checking the section on how to spay cats. Cats were rarely spayed or neutered in the rural areas of Spain. No need to take "God's gift of pleasure" away from them, according to the locals. Logically, it was very responsible of him to double-check the procedure in the textbook. Still, Scott and I cast a worried glance at each other. But Mama was already "under," her fate a question mark.

Mama survived a rough surgery and the bumpy ride back to our farm. She looked so defenseless for a *campo* cat, groggy from anesthesia. Large incision wounds and roughly sewn stitches ran the length of her belly. She was covered with bloody bandages and a paint job of bright red disinfectant. We coddled her and gave her medication, changed her bandages daily, and doused her with the disinfectant the vet had given us until the incisions healed. We spoiled her as she so wanted, but kept her separated from Squeaky. Mama improved and developed a new personality—relaxed—without worries about endless kitten-bearing anymore. Mellow. "I love this life." She even stopped pestering Squeaky so much. Maybe because she didn't feel as vulnerable. Finally, Mama could relax, be fed and watered, feel safe. She had crossed the line from slightly domesticated feral to mostly domesticated. She and Squeaky attained a peaceful coexistence at last.

When we had Mama spayed, we asked the vet to clean out the infected area of her eye while she was still under anesthesia and place sutures as needed in the eyelid to promote healing. We thought the infection had progressed to such an extent that it wouldn't heal without sutures. When we saw Mama after the spay surgery, we were surprised the vet had cleaned the eye wound but didn't suture it. He thought it would heal just using antibiotics. Perhaps the textbook didn't have a section on suturing cats' eyelids in cases like this. I suggested he at least provide a neck cone so we could keep her from licking the surgery wound. Maybe the danger of more infection could be reduced while the open wound healed.

"There aren't any neck cones available in this whole province," he insisted. "We'd have to order one, and it would take weeks to arrive. It's irrelevant anyway; they are totally impractical and dangerous for a farm cat that needs to defend itself."

We should have insisted that the vet suture the eyelid, but that would have required placing Mama under anesthesia again. He thought antibiotics would be sufficient treatment. We felt helpless, unable to get a second opinion.

I rushed to mail close-up photos of Mama's eye to my friend, Diane, in Seattle. She took them to her favorite vet to analyze, although we were all aware it is definitely not standard procedure to prescribe treatment from a photo. The eye infection was very apparent in those photos. The American vet felt the eye should have been cleaned, the eyelid sutured, and a strong course of antibiotics administered. She told Diane, "Make sure they keep the cat on antibiotics. It's her only chance for survival at this point." No other options were available. We administered antibiotic eye drops, potions, and salves to Mama's eye three or four times a day, sometimes tenderly applied by visiting friends from the U.S. who loved Mama's irrepressible spirit. Mama was easy to get attached to, especially the new kinder, gentler Mama!

A construction worker installing kitchen counters in our house came to me one day to warn me, "That cat is very, very sick."

"Yes, we know she's sick. We're treating her with antibiotics. It's the last chance to help her."

He persisted. He didn't think we were being very

smart about Mama's condition. Speaking to me slowly to make sure I understood, and in very unemotional tones, he summed up the situation from his perspective. "I know you like her, but she's not going to get well. You should kill her. I can do it for you."

I knew he couldn't understand why we'd bother to try to save "just a cat," so I simply replied, "Let's see if the antibiotics help."

Mama seemed to sense that we were trying to help her but eventually began to withdraw. She spent her days sleeping quietly outside in the warmth of the sun. The antibiotics were not helping. Squeaky knew something wasn't right. She would approach Mama, not in a hostile way, but to smell her. But, each time, Squeaky recoiled, as if she knew Mama was dying. Mama didn't even react to Squeaky being near.

A few weeks later, this feisty survivor developed a massive staph infection. Oozing, nasty ulcers appeared all over her body. The eye infection had become lethal. No way to save her now. The construction worker's assessment was correct, but his solution was harsh. All in all, though, our gentler solution led to the same end for

Mama. We would have to euthanize Mama or she would become a victim of opportunistic predators because she was so weak. Or she might contaminate the area with staph bacteria, dangerous for Squeaky and for us.

We took Mama back to the vet for the last time, the only time she didn't resist being put in a kennel and riding in the car. She was too weak to struggle. The vet gave her the fatal injection, which usually takes just a few seconds to work. He then left the room so we could say "goodbye." Scott and I petted Mama, trying to avoid the ulcerations on her body. We wanted her to leave this world feeling affection from humans. She surprised us by purring, softly. What a fighter. She wouldn't let go. Ten to fifteen minutes passed. Finally, the vet came back into the room, a little angry. "Why are you petting her? She's consumed by poison, but she's hanging on for you," he said impatiently. When we stopped petting Mama, she died.

Scott painstakingly dug a grave for her in the hard-as-stone dry summer earth under a pine tree on the farm that Mama had claimed as hers. He fashioned a wooden marker and we painted "Mama" on it in her honor. Speaking tenderly to her, we prayed that she would live a new, better life. A few days later, we noticed the marker had toppled. As Scott knelt to fix it, he realized a wild animal had dug Mama out of the ground and eaten her remains. Perhaps that meal was the perpetrator's last, a very toxic one. Justice would have been carried out if he had been the one to gnaw off her eyelid years earlier. We wept that Mama's peaceful resting spot had been defiled. The *campo* had taken her back.

Chapter 7

Go For A Walk?

Squeaky was now undisputed *Reina de la Finca*, free to explore "her" farm unthreatened by vicious feral cats. She began to relax and luxuriate in her surroundings, as she had pre-Mama. We loved the rebirth of her joyful connection to the farm and our lives.

Her first act of sovereignty was to show me that she needed an outdoor vessel for drinking water. We had removed the one close to the house so the feral cats wouldn't come around to drink water and threaten Squeaky. We hadn't bothered to replace it once the feral cats were gone. Squeaky could drink water inside the house, or, when we weren't looking, from the crumbling clay bird bath.

Near the porch was an outdoor faucet positioned above a small cement platform. The platform had an edge about six inches high, and a drain hole. We used the faucet often when working outside, to wash fruit and olives, to fill sprayers with water, for hosing off the patio, for washing dirty hands after field work. It was also a perfect place for me to fill and refill my large plastic mop bucket with water. Mopping chores took a long time, since I had to change the mop water often to get the brick and stone floors clean. I'd often leave the mop bucket at the outside faucet while I switched to a chore that didn't use my scrubbing muscles.

One day, I noticed Squeaky standing on her hind legs, her front paws gripping the rim of the bucket to balance as she peered in to see if she could get some water. "Squeaky! Don't drink that water, it's dirty! You have a water bowl inside, use that." She glared at me, steadying herself again in an attempt to reach the water.

A campo kitty likes to drink water outside, too. This is a great spot because it's near the house but out in the fresh air. What's wrong with a little dirty water, anyway? It's cleaner than the water in that birdbath by the willow tree.

74

"Okay, I have an idea, Squeaky. Wait a minute." I went to the *bodega* and found a new, smaller, blue plastic bucket. "Here, Squeaky, look what I found for you. Your very own bucket."

She came closer as I moved the mop bucket and replaced it with the new blue one. Then I filled it with fresh, cool water, up to the top.

"Try that, sweetie pie."

Well, I liked the other bucket.

She didn't want me to think this switch was easy, so she walked away.

"Okay," I said. "I have to go inside to finish cleaning." Then I peeked out the window to watch her. She walked around the outside of the cement platform, evaluating the bucket.

Better be sure I can drink out of this one.

She couldn't see me spying on her, so up she went, front paws first, clutching the rim of the bucket. Squeaky drank and drank and drank, her tiny, nimble tongue lapping water non-stop.

My own drinking bucket! That's the best water I've had for a long time.

Then off she went for a snooze, so content. That little change, having her own place to drink cool water outside in safety, really meant a lot to her.

I chuckled. "That's fine," I thought. "I can always move her bucket briefly when I need the faucet. Squeaky will be sure to let me know if I forget to put it back. Bless her heart, she's showing me how to add little comforts to her life." We tried to keep her little blue bucket filled with cool water. She used it from then on whenever she was outside.

Squeaky's next priority was to reinstate our favorite pastime, walking the farm property together. No Mama or feral cats to deter us. Just the two of us roaming around, chatting in our respective languages.

I can walk with Carolyn anytime I want to now! Wonder if I'll find a gecko today?

Scott would grin when he saw us take off together, throughout the seasons. Me with a basket in hand to gather treats, Squeaky strolling along right beside me. She'd stop every few minutes and roll on the ground, beckoning me to put down my basket and pet her. I'd obey, then urge her on.

"Squeaky, it's finally spring and time to gather *trigueros* (wild asparagus). You have to help me find some. We'll head up the hill to the stone walls. That's where they usually grow." Summer's hot weather didn't diminish our zest for walking. "Come on, Squeaky, let's pick figs by the old donkey path, and blackberries in the thickets near the old well. You might find some geckos to entertain you."

Cooler fall and winter weather provided lots of interesting walks, too. "Squeaky, let's find some olives to cure for eating. We can play the Olive Game if you get bored." Occasionally, we'd walk through a light dusting of snow to reach our bounty. "Squeaky, I need to gather some pinecones to decorate the fireplace mantel for Christmas. Let's head up the hill to the old pine tree. Do you feel like walking all the way there?"

Squeaky was a perfect *campo* walking companion. She was really quiet, for one thing, except for occasional meows to let me know she was still near me. Sometimes she'd growl to alert me of a perceived threat.

We didn't "talk" a lot. She reminded me that you notice more if you are quiet. Now, I understand that even though you think a cat is sitting idly, just staring into space, it is super-aware of what's going on around it. Analyzing and making plans. Squeaky would be the first to see a green praying mantis clinging to a green grape leaf, perfectly blended for camouflage. Was there a hormone that she sniffed? Did she sense some slight movement? Pounce. A great game even if she missed her prey.

We'd head in a different direction each outing, to enjoy new sights and sounds. Our route depended on whether I was looking for seasonal fruit, nuts, wild oregano for flavoring home-cured olives, or wild iris that bordered our stone walls to make a pretty bouquet for a friend in town.

Sometimes I'd walk with Squeaky because it was hunting season and I didn't like her outside alone. Hunters were prohibited from entering private property, but they did so anyway if they thought no one would object. Scott and I always objected. I'd ask them to leave, explaining that I didn't like them coming to the farm unannounced.

"Our cat might be outdoors. You could accidentally

shoot her instead of whatever animal you are hunting."

"Your *cat?*" they'd laugh, leaving me even more nervous. They didn't seem to care if she got in the line of fire.

Mostly, we took safe walks and had lots of fun together. We ended up favoring two special places on the farm for our walking adventures. The *era* and the old donkey path. An *era* is a large flat threshing structure built to facilitate the crushing and windblown separation of wheat chaff and/or bean husks, like garbanzos. They were very useful before farm work was mechanized. *Eras* were always constructed at an open and elevated location to maximize the available wind currents.

The huge, neglected, hand-built *era* on our farm was in a large hilly field at the end of the property farthest from the front gate. It was a circular exposed rock platform jutting out from a hill. Its downhill circular supporting wall, measuring about six feet high by two feet deep by twenty feet in diameter, was made of hand-stacked slate, without mortar. Tons of dirt and rocks were back-filled into the empty area in the middle to support the massive rough slate wall and to create a level working surface—also covered with slate rock.

When we first moved to the farm, it was almost impossible to see the *era* from a distance because it was hidden by overgrown weeds, blackberry brambles, and loose stones that had washed down from the hill above in seasonal storms.

The previous owner had dug a rough pit on the downside of the *era* to catch water run-off that could damage the stone walls and olive trees below.

We rarely walked to the *era*. The path was overrun by prickly thistles in the summer, too soupy and slippery in rainy weather. Even Squeaky didn't find the path appealing.

Scott and I knew we couldn't clear the whole field surrounding the *era* with our weed-eaters and clippers, as we had cleared other spots on our farm. When at last we bought a tractor, after almost three years of clearing by hand, Scott could finally plow the field. Then we could get near the *era* with the weed-eater and start clearing brambles. It took us days of hard work to cut and burn all the brambles and weeds that literally covered every inch of the massive *era*.

What a thrill it was, the day we stood on top of that enormous stone structure, high on a hill, celebrating the liberation of the *era*. The bucolic view was a perfect panorama of bygone days in rural Spain. Quaint, slate stone walls wound down our valley and continued through another, framing old dirt paths and, occasionally, rustic stone farmhouses.

Acre after acre of olive trees, oak trees, and fig trees dotted the rolling hills. No electric lines or poles distracted from the view. Rarely were cars driven on those narrow roads. The only sounds, other than wind and rain, were from occasional hikers chatting as they walked the old paths, or a shepherd walking with his flock of sheep, their melodious bells tinkling.

Finally able to see my way around the area, I realized there were two lone, small olive trees on one side. They were *cornicabras*, their fruit shaped a bit like the horn of a goat—thick in the middle, becoming elongated and curved at the tip. Why were there only two olive trees on this part of the farm? Had other olive trees been removed to make room for the *era* and only these two remained? Or had these two once been planted there to take advantage of the moisture created by the water running down the hill?

I asked the shepherd who grazed his sheep at our farm about the history of these two trees. He often solved little mysteries for us because he had lived in the area his whole life and knew the fields like the back of his hand. But this time, the answer was, "*No sé* (I don't know). Maybe the other trees washed away."

Sometimes it seemed like he just didn't want to get into long explanations, so *No sé* was his way of ending the question-and-answer session.

The two trees were in need of a severe pruning and thinning, but were still producing some fruit. I saw shriveled, fallen olives beneath them. I asked Scott to prune the trees to stimulate olive production for future harvests.

Squeaky had also tried to navigate through that field before we cleared it, always returning home with a coat full of stickers, thistle heads, poppy pods. Too many obstacles for a fun romp. However, after we pruned the two trees and cleared the field, which we continued to do every year, Squeaky loved to go with me on a walk to the *era* for a quick game of Chase the Olive. Then—sniff, sniff, sniff—new things to discover. Depending on the season, she'd stare at caterpillars, persecute geckos, toy with earthworms, pester toads, catch mice and voles, or nibble young green grass (kitty herbal tonic). While I worked nearby, she would sit atop the *era* for hours, almost hypnotized by barn swallows darting and sweeping overhead.

Boy! Are they fast! But they dip and zigzag all around. I don't know if I can catch one of these.

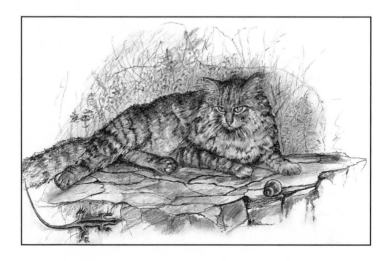

Many times, we headed out to the *era* to check out the showcase of birds of prey riding the air currents. Eagles, black buzzards with powerful beaks, hawks, falcons. Squeaky watched them carefully, staying close to me.

I hope they keep going, over to another farm. They make me nervous.

The old donkey path was the original entrance to the property. Day laborers nearly a century ago would arrive with donkeys to work the fields, tend grapevines, prune trees, pick olives or fruit, make wine. Livestock could be herded down this path for seasonal grazing. The narrow, irregular path was dirt and stone. On either side were hand-stacked slate stone walls, about four feet high, curving down toward the almond tree near the house.

A friend from Madroñera came often to re-stack or re-build those precious ancient stone walls. It's an art form to stack the stones efficiently, using no cement to stabilize them. Sometimes the shepherd would repair them, too, if many stones were dislodged when his sheep took a shortcut over the wall.

Magnificent native Holm oak trees lined one side of the path. These oaks produce the *bellota* acorns in fall, which are free-range food for Spain's coveted *ibérico* pigs. Perhaps our pigpen was once shelter for *ibérico* pigs, though it was empty when we moved there. Intermingled among the Holm oaks were cork trees, also in the oak family, their thick bark "peeled" every ten years for cork industries, including wine corks. Fig trees, about five varieties, lined the opposite wall, providing sweet fruit to further supplement the diet of the *ibéricos*, whose meat is renowned for its sweet, nutty flavor.

Fig trees all over the property produced an abundance of fleshy, succulent fruit for human enjoyment as well. My favorite spot to pick figs was by the old donkey path. Unusual varieties were there, like the small, delicate-skinned yellow figs with red centers. They tasted like honey when ripe. Squeaky liked to join me as I gathered an assortment of fresh figs on hot summer days. She'd flop down in the shade beneath the tree, while I circled around picking only the perfectly ripe, ready-to-eat *(en su punto)* figs. One of our neighbors showed me that figs are *en su punto* when the stem bends away from the branch and the fruit slumps. You barely need to touch the stem, and the fig detaches. You can't always judge ripeness by color, because some varieties don't change color as they ripen. Bent stems are almost always an indication of a fig that's ready to be enjoyed.

"Yummmm, Squeaky. I know what Scott and I are having for dinner tonight. Toasted country bread with olive oil, *ibérico* cured ham slices, and fresh figs. Doesn't that sound good, Squeaky?"

I think I'll go look for a gecko. A tapa (snack, appetizer) *sounds better to me.*

Squeaky loved to walk on the old path with me, whatever the season. She usually spied something of interest tucked into the stone walls: geckos, mice, lizards, grasshoppers. If not, she'd let me know it was Play Time.

Maybe I can get her to play. I'll look under the almond tree for a shell.

Discarded empty almond shells, weathered and lightweight, were great toys. No clean up was necessary outdoors. I'd toss a shell to her, she'd jump in the air like a basketball player, and hit it back to me! If she missed it, I'd find another almond shell to throw. When

Squeaky got bored, she'd climb into the crook of the old almond tree and stare at me.

Think of something else to play.

I'd find something flexible, like a small green twig to tease her so she could bat at it from different positions in the crook of the tree. Such perfect, simple entertainment. The game usually ended when I grabbed her off her perch to give her a big hug. "Oh, Squeaky, you are so much fun! Come on, let's see what else we can find. Are you hungry?"

Oh, yeah. I forgot about my tapa.

I loved the freedom we shared, able to walk, "talk," and enjoy each other's company without threats from Mama and the feral cats. Squeaky seemed thoroughly attuned to her surroundings, no longer distracted by Mama's threatening behavior.

She followed Scott around in the vineyard, too, sitting close to him as he restored the old vines to health, one by one.

Over one hundred years old, the vines had weathered blights and inclement weather, and many of the trunks were full of termites. Scott methodically walked from vine to vine, season after season, removing the termites, cleaning away the decayed bark, giving the vines new energy to produce better fruit. It was tedious work, but his persistence paid off. The hobby wine he made from those vines was an excellent field blend of *garnacha*, *tempranillo*, and *cariñena* red wine varietals. He also made a small quantity of white table wine from the only two white grape varietals on the farm, *alorije* and *blanqueta*.

Sometimes, when Scott was working in the vineyard, he'd take a break with Squeaky. They would sit on the ground near the vines "talking" about what needed to be done next. Squeaky is a very good listener, but she always gets back to basics. A Squeaky roll in the dirt followed by a snuggle not only brightened Scott's spirits, but re-affirmed her *Reina de la Finca* status.

We three were close again, nurtured by our evolving attachment to each other and to Lagar La Señora. Sadly, it was to be a short-lived contentment for all of us. Squeaky, who would rather cuddle than fight, was forced to defend her territory yet again. This time, it was a dangerous male feral cat. Young, strong, and nasty. Not soft around the edges like Mama. Was he one of Mama's numerous offspring returning to his birthplace? We had never seen him before, nor had our neighbors. What led this menacing animal to our farm?

We called him "Peli," short for *peligroso* (dangerous), for his appearance and demeanor. Peli was unusually large for a feral cat, easily recognizable because of his sinister physical characteristics. A misshapen bobbed tail was grim evidence of his brutal lifestyle. Glistening, menacing topaz eyes revealed an aggressive nature. The cartilage at the top of his left ear was torn, so his ear flopped down on that side. His fur was medium length, gray with a bluish cast. We guessed he was about three years old and had spent a lot of that time fighting for survival and dominance.

Our farm was full of potential for a good life from his point of view. Lots of little animals to catch. Water. Even the bonus of a big house for shelter. Only Squeaky stood in his way.

He'd usually approach her at dusk, just testing her vigilance at first. When she'd notice him and practice her newly acquired hissing/threatening vocal technique learned from Mama and the feral cats, he'd retreat for a short distance. The next step was to intimidate her. Get closer. Crouch and growl, then lunge at her. She'd hold her ground and shriek. We'd hear her and come running to chase him away. Poor Squeaky, all she wanted was a quiet life in the country. So did we.

Had Scott and I not been vigilant, it would have been easy for Peli to overpower Squeaky. We couldn't let that happen. We made sure she was safe inside the house whenever we left the farm. When we were there, it was the three of us against Peli.

Scott summed up our frustration one day after chasing Peli for the umpteenth time. "Too bad there are no Trap/Neuter/Return services around here for feral cats. Anyway, Peli is too wily to ever be trapped. Plus, he's here for a while, and then just seems to disappear for a week or so. We think he's left the area, but just when we're least expecting it, he returns to stalk Squeaky."

Chapter 8

Starry Nights

Every night, just before bedtime, the generator had to be turned off. Squeaky liked to come along as Scott and I scurried down the driveway toward the generator shed, flashlight in hand. Regardless of the weather—rain, sleet, wind, occasional snow, or often, quite beautiful conditions—it was the pre-bedtime ritual.

The generator ran for three hours on one tank of fuel; after that, we had to add more fuel or turn it off so as not to damage the motor. We paced our indoor, nighttime activities around this three-hour plan. So did Squeaky, knowing that "last call" to come inside for the night was when the generator was turned off.

Once darkness fell on Lagar La Señora, we needed the power of the generator to operate our indoor lights and the laptop computer. We'd eat a quick dinner and spend hours of computer time trying to get online using our *teléfono rural* (rural telephone) to answer e-mails or search for information. The rural telephone looked like a landline phone but functioned like a cell phone. There was a cell phone tower in town, and a roof antenna on our house. The signal was stronger for the *teléfono rural* than for our small cell phone which had poor-to-no coverage in our valley. Even so, the signal to the rural phone was often weak, or intermittent, challenging us to stay online long enough to send and receive messages. It was predictably frustrating.

Our three hours of generator use passed all too quickly. Grumbling about our online connection issues, or some other seemingly insurmountable problem, we'd sprint hastily out the door toward the generator shed only to stop in our tracks as we witnessed the silent, magical, starry, starry world above us. No street lights to dim the beauty of the constellations or full moon on a cloudless night. So close, so bright. A heavenly light show twinkling in the silence. If we had not needed to go outside to turn off the generator, we'd have remained in the house, self-absorbed with our little dilemmas. We would have missed many of these splendid moments. Perfectly delineated Orion, Big and Little Dippers, The Milky Way. Each constellation steadily leading you to the next. Quiet, timeless sky. God's presence illuminating our path.

Squeaky would roll around in the dirt driveway, squirming and wiggling, linked to the earth and the sky. She loved the night and probably wondered on spectacular nights like these why we stayed inside so long. I've heard that cats don't perceive a difference in light and darkness, but Squeaky's actions seemed to counter this theory. On overcast nights, she would come inside with us. Full moons seemed to compel her to stay outside all night. Her instincts told her when it would be clear at night—best to sleep a little more during the day in anticipation of her nighttime shift.

Squeaky chose her viewpoint carefully, studiously, over time. The tiptop of one section of the house roof not only provided her with an extraordinary view of her

Kitty Kingdom, but kept most night predators away from her. She figured out how to jump onto a small, flat slate stone jutting out from the *bodega* wall, then navigate the steep buttress of the house. From there, she'd cautiously make her way onto the roof, calculating her steps so as not to move the clay roof tiles or attract attention. The end of the roof was her favorite viewpoint, providing an almost 360-degree view of the farm. Stealthy, nighttime, covert maneuvers.

Squeaky was safe there from most animals, in a prime spot to watch the late night parade of mice and voles, wild boar, foxes, owls, skunks, intruder cats and dogs. The first time I realized Squeaky was on the roof, after calling her for more than an hour and fearing she was hurt, I called her name again, adding, "So there you are, you little sneak."

She turned to look at me with an expression that said, "P-lease be quiet; this is my *hiding* spot." She looked so regal, so perfectly feline on her observation point, that I was sorry to have broken the spell. I was relieved to know she was safe up there, though in awe of her innate ability to figure out where best to perch.

She had evaluated her space, choosing the safest spot from which to study her territory.

Sometimes Squeaky stayed on the roof all night in spite of my efforts to lure her into the house. When she wouldn't come inside, I never slept well, hyper-aware of every unfamiliar noise. We worried that Peli would discover her rooftop observation point. We never knew when he would re-appear. He kept us off-guard by disappearing for short periods. Every day it became part of our routine to check the fields for his presence. If we relaxed, thinking he was no longer a threat, sure enough, he would return.

As Fate would have it, Peli was the only animal who figured out how to get on the roof. He probably observed Squeaky's routine night after night. Very late one night we heard Squeaky's shrieks from on the roof, followed by sounds of a growling cat running, and loosening the roof tiles.

"It's probably Peli," Scott and I yelled at the same time. We quickly rolled out of bed, grabbed the ever-present flashlight, and bolted to the front door. "Damn it, he found her hiding spot!"

Right then, both cats jumped off the roof, landing hard on the ground in front of us. Squeaky ran to her Last Chance High Ground Haven, the tall willow tree in front of the house. Usually she could escape pursuing animals this way; in fact, she had often climbed the tree to escape Mama's bad temper.

Mama didn't have very good depth perception because of her mutilated eyelid, so she wasn't comfortable climbing trees. Thus, the willow tree became Squeaky's safe spot. But Peli was a Seek and Destroy Missile! He chased her up the tree, way too high. Squeaky panicked and fled farther, out onto a small, weak branch.

We feared she would lose her balance and crash to the ground, injuring herself seriously, or worse.

Peli edged closer to her, not about to give up now. Scott and I clapped our hands loudly, yelling, *"Fuera* (get away)" several times hoping the loudness would scare him. Squeaky was still trying to keep her balance on the branch, afraid to go backwards because Peli was there. Our noise strategy spooked Peli. He cautiously backtracked down the long trunk of the tree. Once closer to the ground, he leapt to his getaway. I chased him, throwing a rock in his direction to scare him even farther away, while Scott stood by the tree, hoping Squeaky wouldn't jump from that height. Scott knew he had to talk her down from the willow tree branch.

"Okay, Squeaky, pay attention. You can't jump down, you'll get hurt. You have to walk backwards on the branch until you can turn around without falling. You can do it." She looked at him, totally focused, assessing her options. Afraid to move, Squeaky clung to the tiny branch. "Come on, Squeaky, you're a *campo* kitty now; just use your claws to hold on. When you feel the branch get bigger, then you can turn around."

Well, at least Peli is gone. I'll try to do what Scott says.

Squeaky managed to backtrack on that little branch, holding on for dear life with her two front paws, then righting herself. To our great relief, she reached the ground safely. She was still a little agitated and quite embarrassed but went inside with us, limping just a little. As I approached the front door of the house, I glanced out over the field again, and there was Peli, studying us from a safe distance. Another sleepless night but Squeaky had dodged the Peli Bullet again. She didn't stay out late at night very often after that incident.

Peli didn't give up. He stalked Squeaky again shortly after the willow tree incident. She was way out in the field, far from the house. Scott and I were out of sight. Peli must have thought this was his perfect moment to rid the Lagar of Squeaky. He wouldn't wait for the cover of darkness this time. Did she sense his presence before he lunged at her? Or was she sleeping under the shade of an olive tree, comfortable and cool on this hot, sunny, still day, unaware of his approach?

We heard the piercing screams from the far end of

the farm where we were pruning olive tree suckers. "It must be Peli; he's cornered her again!"

Simultaneously we dropped our pruners and hurried to the scene. Our fears of another attack were realized. "Scott, I'll go ahead. Your hip has been really sore lately, so don't run."

But he did run.

Did Squeaky wonder if we would appear to protect her? Or fear that we weren't close enough to help? We could see she was in automatic defense mode, fighting Peli valiantly, instinctively, as we raced toward her. How long could she defend herself? She was no match for his youth and power.

By the time we reached her, Squeaky was on her back, too weak to fight Peli any longer. Her shrill cries were her only remaining defense as he ripped open her belly with his sharp claws. When he saw us, he fled. I know I would have killed him if I had caught him. I sobbed as I knelt in the parched soil to get a close look at our beloved kitty.

Squeaky lay dazed and wounded, panting rapidly after the fight. We approached her cautiously, not knowing if she would try to run, or if she was able to respond to us. We spoke her name softly, repeatedly.

"Squeaky, Squeaky; it's okay. Peli can't hurt you anymore. We'll take care of you." We waited briefly to touch her, not wanting to trigger a fight response. Both of us were silently praying our sweet friend would be okay, one more time. Somehow, she seemed aware enough to know she was safe again and that we were there. She seemed comforted by our presence. She let Scott lift her up tenderly. He staggered, hindered by his weak hip. No matter, Squeaky needed him. Her wound didn't seem life-threatening, but her belly was bloody. We didn't know if she had internal injuries.

"Let's take her to the house to clean her up a little, then head for the vet's office," I said, mentally calculating the time of day, whether his office would be closed for siesta, how long it would take us to get there. Scott held her close as I walked beside them, keeping my eye out for Peli. What a sight—two dusty, sweaty Americano farmers carrying a helpless, bloody cat to safety in 100-degree heat.

We stumbled over the rocky terrain and down the

hill between the irregular rows of olive trees. At the old abandoned pigpen, we began our steep ascent toward the house. We rushed past the willow tree and burst through the thick wooden doors of our sanctuary to coolness and safety. Squeaky remained motionless, but her eyes were open.

"We'll take care of our sweet kitty. Let us help you," I said, choking back tears. "You were smart to yell so loud. We were a long way from you."

We quickly applied hydrogen peroxide to the wound, grabbed the kennel, laid her on a clean towel that experience taught us to keep emergency-ready, and were off to the vet, yet again. I sat beside her kennel in the back seat of our car, determined to keep her connected to us, not to Peli's attack. Scott maneuvered our car on the bumpy road as fast as he could.

Forcing my voice to be steady and calm, I kept talking to her. "Squeaky, you fought well because you had to. That was a close one, wasn't it? I am so glad we got to you in time to help." Over and over I reassured her, "You'll be better soon."

I silently prayed that would be true.

Even the vet was disconcerted when we arrived with Squeaky. "Oh! No! Was she in a fight?" he asked. "Let's take a look." He spoke soothingly to Squeaky this time. *"Ay, pobrecita. ¿Qué te pasó Es-qui-ki?* (Poor little thing. What happened to you, Squeaky?)"

While he cleaned the wounds and painted them with red disinfectant, I filled him in on Squeaky's latest and worst attack by Peli. Luckily, Squeaky needed only three large stitches, done with topical anesthesia, and the always-prescribed dose of antibiotics. Internal injuries were ruled out after a quick exam. The vet's office didn't have x-ray equipment, so we had to assume Squeaky did not have any broken bones. We would need to watch her for any unusual symptoms.

"What a relief she didn't need major surgery," I said to the vet, when Squeaky was ready to go home.

"Yes," he replied in a very serious tone, "she was lucky you were there to save her. But it will be different the next time. Peli is a feral male cat smart about surviving in the *campo.* Now he knows he is stronger than *Es-qui-ki.* He will keep attacking her until he kills her. That is the way it is."

104

Scott and I looked at each other in despair. The vet confirmed our worst fears for Squeaky's safety. How could we continue to protect her? Peli definitely had murder on his mind.

"What if we can catch him and bring him to you to be neutered? Then, maybe he'd be less violent."

"Catch him?" the vet challenged. "You'll never be able to catch or trap him. And I wouldn't get near him even if you brought him here. That kind of cat is too dangerous to deal with. You'd better just keep *Es-qui-ki* away from him."

We returned to Lagar La Señora with heavy hearts. Squeaky survived Peli's attack this time, but what did the future hold for her? How could we protect her without keeping her inside all the time? First, we had to make sure she recovered from Peli's attack by faithfully applying disinfectant to her wounds and giving her the prescribed antibiotics for the recommended number of days. We worried that she might try to pull out the stitches in her belly with her teeth, but she was smart enough not to do that. We snuggled her and sweet-talked her even more than usual, realizing that we had almost lost her. "We're family, Squeaky. We have to take care of each other."

What a relief that Squeaky's recovery from her wounds was speedy. She looked so frail and helpless when we brought her home after the vet visit that it was hard to imagine she'd be back to normal anytime soon. But Squeaky quickly returned to her outdoor lifestyle, perhaps just a tiny bit more guarded than she had been before the attack.

Where is Peli? I hope he never comes around again. He's too tough for me.

It wasn't long before Squeaky's love of roaming around *her* farm erased any trace of worry she had about Peli reappearing. But Scott and I faithfully kept a watchful eye when Squeaky was outside, just in case Peli returned.

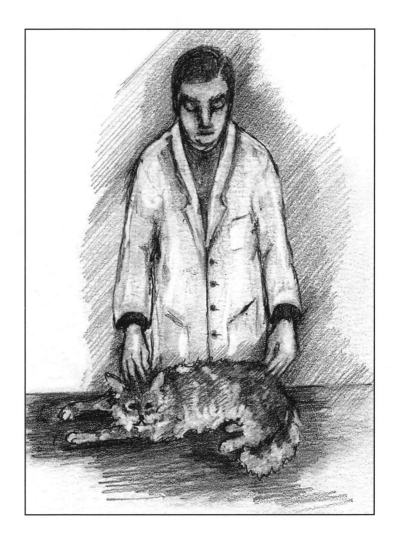

Chapter 9

Look Into My Eyes

On summer mornings, we rarely found time to linger over a cherished homemade *café con leche* (espresso coffee with steamed milk). The hottest weather stretched from mid-May until the end of September, making it essential to begin chores early, at six or seven o'clock in the morning. Forget turning on the generator to run the fancy electric espresso machine we brought with us to Spain. No time to enjoy Scott's exceptional espresso-making talents. Just a simple twist-pot espresso for us, prepared on the butane-fueled kitchen stove.

We'd hurry outside, not wanting to waste any of the cool temperature, and work until two o'clock in the afternoon, lunch time. Sometimes we quit working at noon because the temperature soared to well over 100 degrees. The sun was migraine bright. Our bodies needed water and the blessed sanctuary of the thick house walls.

We'd find Squeaky snoozing under the canopy of a grapevine, smart enough not to be hunting or playing in the intense heat. She became listless and dehydrated if we left her there, so one of us would crawl under the grapevine to retrieve her. She always resisted being forced to return to the house.

Don't drag me out from my hiding place and make me go inside. I'm not ready!

But once inside, she'd drink water and flop down on the cool stone floor to refresh herself. Cat bath, then a snooze. Her dinnertime was later, after we came inside again. It was easier to entice her from nighttime adventures if she hadn't eaten during the day. Well, maybe a gecko tail or a small grasshopper. Kitty *tapas*.

When the days were oppressively hot and we had to return to the fields after siesta, Scott and I ate light lunches. Sometimes a cup of leftover cold gazpacho or a piece of *tortilla de patatas* (Spanish potato/onion omelet). If you're not too full, it's easier to work in the heat and do the chores that require lots of bending over. In July, it was a major bending task to place bird netting over the grapevines and anchor them with rocks from the fields. Pruning olive suckers from the base of olive trees in August/September required bending over, too, as did collecting figs that had fallen to the ground and dried.

After a long, mostly unrestful siesta during the hottest part of the day, the three of us would return to the fields around seven o'clock in the evening. Scott and I to work, Squeaky to hunt for geckos, her renewable toys of preference. She would hunt them, bite off their tails, release them, and munch on her *tapa*. Neighbors reassured us that gecko tails regenerate, but we could only hope the surgery wasn't painful.

When we returned to the fields, the sun would be lower in the sky but still strong. The air remained furnace hot. The ambient temperature would get cooler the longer we worked. When Squeaky was bored or lonely, she'd find us and roll around in the dirt until we took a break and played with her. She always helped keep our priorities in perspective. Just the sight of her walking over to greet us was like getting a big hug when we needed it most. Sometimes we'd work as late as eleven o'clock, when at last darkness fell. The air was just beginning to get cool and breezy, refreshing at last. Forced to stop working, we'd sit under an olive tree for a while with Squeaky, the three of us coming back to life again.

One day, after Squeaky's normal playtime in the farm's wild kingdom, she returned to the house for a nap. As usual, she "bathed" herself first. Cats like pre-activity bathing and post-activity bathing, a very busy, cleanly life. This time, the "activity" was a nap. Squeaky was a fastidious bather. Better to bathe lots instead of being grabbed on the way into the house after a fun day in the dirt to be brushed and combed by Carolyn the Clean Machine. When I'd open the door to let her inside, she learned to slink backwards as a precaution while she made sure I didn't have a brush in my hand.

I might need to escape. Better be ready.

Many times, I let her get away with it. With so many chores to do, sometimes I had to catch up to her later.

I watched as she leapt purposefully onto her favorite chair of the week. That would be the chair with a large padded seat cushion plus a bonus back cushion so that she could "power bathe" all areas of her body, stretching here and there as necessary, always supported by a cushion. Squeaky's long-haired, earth-sweeping body was like a dirt, bug, and debris magnet in the fields, so her super-effective tongue got a big workout in dry, dusty weather. A good self-bathing session could last an hour in summer and was repeated after each of her many daily outings. Often, I'd sneak up on her while she was bathing, brush in hand.

"Squeaky, I'll just brush you a little bit to help you out, then you can continue."

She'd tolerate the brushing for a minute or two, then shift positions and growl at me. Pretty soon we'd be in a control contest. It was a great game to her to figure out how to get out of it. Jump off the chair in a huff, run under a bed, just out of reach? Fall asleep immediately after bathing? Bolt out the door when Scott opened it to enter the house?

All that brushing and combing hurts my skin. Just let

me do it my way.

"Squeaky, what's the matter with your eye?"

She was licking her paw and bathing her right eye, repetitiously, almost anxiously. I glanced quickly at the eye, and saw nothing that could be irritating it. "Must have been a really dusty adventure today. At least this time of year, it's not because you jumped into stinging nettles again." What a blessing she wasn't thrashing around wildly. Nonetheless, living on the farm taught us in a very profound way the lesson of consequence if things are overlooked. I made a mental note to keep track of how often she bathed her eye.

Days later, it still seemed to be bothering her. Scott and I looked closely and saw nothing in the eye or eyelid. We used some mild eyewash drops to try to purge the mystery irritant and hoped for the best. For a day or so, she seemed better.

If I act normal, they'll leave me alone.

Except, she still obsessively "washed" that eye. Countless times, Scott held her while I looked into her eye with a magnifying glass, trying to see if something was imbedded. We couldn't find a thing, but we could tell Squeaky didn't feel good. We'd come inside between farm chores to check on her, just to make sure she was okay. She responded with purrs, but didn't want to go outside much. A few days later, she was eating less, sleeping lots, and still obsessively washing her eye.

"Oh, Scott, this is horrible. Squeaky just got over Peli's brutal attack and now she's ailing again. Maybe we never should have brought her here. It seems like we've condemned her to a life of ill health and danger." I was distraught.

"I know," he replied, his face tense with concern. "It sure is an uphill battle for Squeaky. But let's find out if it's something simple this time before we over-react."

Once again we were off to see the vet, who examined Squeaky's eye, looking for visual signs of infection. He proclaimed that nothing was wrong. "Probably just a minor irritation."

"Minor irritation?" I snapped. "There must be something in her eye. She washes it constantly with her paw."

Unfazed by my concern, he responded, "She'll be fine. Her biggest problem is that feral male cat. Don't worry so much about these little things. Cats can take care of themselves."

"Great," I thought. "That's so reassuring." But I knew something was in her eye.

Back to the farm we three went. Soon, Squeaky lost interest in everything other than eating a little food now and then, sleeping, and bathing her eye. She seemed to prefer the safety of the house.

Never would we have imagined the magnitude of Squeaky's suffering. Cats don't whimper or follow you around meowing when they are scared and hurting. They cope until it is impossible to cope. Then they withdraw. And if they withdraw, it's usually too late to help them. It was a blessing to be connected in spirit with Squeaky. To sense that "something" was wrong, to make sure we watched her, trying to analyze and take corrective action, since she couldn't fix it herself. Although she had stopped washing her eye so much, we could see pain, a dullness, in her eye. Not her usual sparkling expression.

I was so frustrated. "What can we do to help her?" I begged for an answer from Scott, who couldn't figure it out either. "We know she's miserable," I added, "but, what's causing the problem? The vet doesn't seem to take this seriously. We've looked into her eye hundreds of times and can't see anything stuck in it. I wish Squeaky could just tell us what's wrong. She's *familia* and needs our help." We realized, again, that her fate rested in our hands.

A few days later, Squeaky marched up to Scott when he was standing near the window in the bedroom. He loved the second-floor bird's eye view of the fields, a good spot for assessing work completed and projects to be started. She seemed to want him to pick her up. He did so. Anything to please our little sweetie.

"Squeaky, what can we do to help you? We hate to see you suffer so much." As usual, he glanced at her eye, expecting by now to find nothing. Instead, he noticed a very small "something" sticking up from her lower lid.

"Carolyn, come here with the flashlight, quick! I think there's something stuck in Squeaky's eyelid!"

I grabbed the flashlight and headed up the stairs to the bedroom. Squeaky was beginning to squirm a little.

Oh, no, don't make a big deal out of this; I just wanted you to see what's wrong.

She didn't try to escape, letting us shine the light in her eye. This time, yes, we could see a faint trace of something, still unidentifiable. Teeny tip of who knows what. It wasn't long enough for us to use tweezers to pull it out. We certainly didn't want to risk damaging her eye even more with unskilled attempts to remove it. The only choice was to head for the vet's office, again. It was a bit of a sinking feeling. Would the vet be peeved or helpful? No matter, it was our only chance to help Squeaky.

The vet seemed a little irked when we rushed into his office.

Here are those foreigners again with that spoiled cat, he probably thought. But he agreed, that, yes, by golly, there was something teeny protruding from Squeaky's lower eyelid. "All right," he sighed, "let's take a look." The vet took a large pair of tweezers, probably used for dogs, since cats can take care of themselves, and zeroed in on Squeaky's eyelid as we held her tight. Squeaky was terrified. She didn't know what kind of object was coming toward her eye. I could feel her heart pounding. The vet persisted, managing to get the tweezers around "it."

"Oh, it's probably just a little thorn or something," he muttered, sounding bored. He pulled and pulled some more. "Good grief! This is huge!" the vet announced, a little more interested now. Squeaky was as still as she could be. Perhaps she realized that at last the problem was found and someone was helping her.

After what seemed like an eternity—but was probably just seconds—the vet yanked out the frightful thorn and showed it to us. How could such a large piece of thorn have been embedded in her eyelid for so long? How much pain must she have tolerated? Why couldn't we see the thorn in the first place?

"Why couldn't you find it before?" I challenged the vet.

He explained that cats have two lower eyelids; only one is easily visible to humans. The thorn had embedded itself into the "invisible" eyelid and slowly erupted, which was why we couldn't see anything for a long time. I wondered if Squeaky's obsessive bathing of the area had served to drive the thorn deeper instead of releasing it. At this point, it didn't matter. Our little friend would feel better now. Even the vet was amazed that Squeaky had been coping with worsening discomfort for weeks. He washed out the eyelid and recommended the cure-all medication, antibiotics, to ward off infection. "See?" the vet concluded, "No big deal. Just a thorn."

"Just a cat," I thought.

We conjectured that Squeaky had probably jumped off a stone wall into a mound of thistles or a blackberry thicket in pursuit of a *tapa*—gecko, mouse, grasshopper. Knowing her, she probably caught her target, played with it, maybe ate it and then thought, *Ouch! What's wrong with my eye? Better bathe it really well when I get back to the house.*

The trip back to the Lagar was lighthearted for all three of us. Squeaky seemed to feel better already; Scott and I certainly did. "Squeaky, you were very brave. That thorn must have hurt you a lot." Amazingly, there were no traces of infection. A slight redness near the point of entry, but no pus in the eyelid, nor swelling. What if Squeaky hadn't marched up to Scott to let him see her eye just at the right time? What if Scott hadn't paid attention to Squeaky when she trusted him enough to show him? Fortunately, we were all paying attention to each other. Ever guided by the "consequence theme," though, we made sure we kept her on antibiotics for the necessary period. Haunting memories of Mama's eye infection and the tragic outcome always reminded us that Squeaky's well-being depended on us.

Chapter 10

Babysitting Blues

Scott and I assumed that it would be relatively simple to kennel Squeaky when we needed to travel to the United States. We had been told by the locals in the pueblo that there were kennels in the area. We anticipated yearly trips to the U.S. to visit our families. It wasn't an option to take her with us, dragging her back and forth through the international airline travel loop, so we probably would have to kennel Squeaky, but not often.

We were shocked to discover, soon after settling down on the farm, that the "kennels" our Spanish friends referred to were only for dogs. No cat kennels existed in the whole province. Now we had to be creative. Thus began the perpetual, worrisome saga of trying to find reliable "sitters" for Squeaky when Scott and I went on a long trip without her. For what seemed like an eternity, the solution eluded us.

Sometimes, we would alternate solo trips to the U.S. so that one of us could stay with Squeaky. That way, at least part of her *familia* was with her. It was worth it to us to do that so she could have her normal indoor/outdoor life and not stress like she did when we were both leaving. She usually panicked when she saw suitcases being packed.

We're not going on a plane trip again, are we?

But she calmed down once she realized one of us would stay with her, enjoying the one-on-one time.

When Scott returned from the first solo trip to the U.S., Squeaky and I were really glad to have him back on the farm. All together again. It was such a good feeling. A big project awaited us—hand-scything of tall weeds along the driveway, around the olive trees, and in the vineyard.

The bush-pruned (not trellised) grapevines, the

olive trees, and fruit trees were all intermingled in the small rustic farm style of planting, not arranged in straight lines for easy access and harvesting as they are today in most commercial farms. It was difficult to tend them except by walking through with hand tools or hiring someone from the pueblo to bring his mule to pull a single-bottom plow. We realized we were going to need motorized weed-eaters, chain saws and even a tractor eventually, but the first year or two we wanted to see if we could do most of the tasks by hand. It was arduous work, but by doing that for a few years, we really got a good feeling for the lay of the land.

Scott and I would spend weeks slowly making our way through the fields, scything and raking, and stacking the weeds to collect later. There were so many tall weeds that Squeaky, loving to follow us around when we worked, would lose sight of us. She couldn't see us from her level low on the ground, but she figured out if she climbed up an olive tree and sat in the crook where the trunk meets the first large branches, she'd have a broader view.

Where the heck are they? They should talk more when

they work so I can hear where they are. I'll meow so they can find me.

We'd sometimes not be able to see her, but we could hear her meowing, so we'd walk over to where she was, lift her out of the tree and carry her to where we were working. Then we'd put her in the crook of an olive tree close to us. We didn't mind personally transporting her to our location; it kept her from getting entangled in so many thistles and weeds.

When we began planning our first non-emergency trip together to the U.S. to see family early the next year, we still hadn't found anyone Squeaky trusted enough to care for her while we were gone. She seemed wary of our Spanish acquaintances from the pueblo when they came to visit, as if she couldn't predict their behavior. Perhaps the sound of the Spanish language confused her; I know their abrupt movements and loud voices did. She'd usually hide in the house, or outside in a favorite hiding spot until they left. She was quiet like us. She liked walking in the fields, noticing things you don't notice when everyone is talking and joking. A classical music fan, fiercely independent, a little standoffish and persnickety, but with a wicked sense of humor and a heart of gold. "Oh, Squeaky," I thought to myself many times, "we three are quite a match."

A little reluctantly, but graciously, the previous owners of the Lagar, "Mama's" first family, offered to take care of Squeaky while we were gone. We made them promise not to let Squeaky outside, fearing she would run away. They thought we were being cruel, but promised. This would be Squeaky's first experience alone at the Lagar without at least one of us to make her feel loved and secure. She nervously watched both of us pack suitcases.

What's going on? Not the airplane again!

She could feel the tension related to our journey no matter how nonchalant we tried to act.

Maybe they're leaving me! I'll hide outside.

She'd stay outside longer each night, ignoring us when she finally came in..

If they're leaving me, I have to get used to taking care of myself.

We tried to comfort her, talking to her as we held her close.

"Squeaky, don't panic. Scott and I are going on a trip for three weeks. The good news is that you don't have to go with us and be on a plane again. We've made sure there will be someone here every day to take care of you. You'll have to be a good kitty though. Behave yourself with our friends. They are doing us all a big favor. But you'll have to make some adjustments. You won't be able to go outside while we're gone. "

The whole time? Are you kidding?

"As soon as we come home, you can go outside again. Come on, give us a little snuggle, please." She started to purr, then thought better of it, jumping out of my arms.

Why won't you stay here with me?

She walked across the room in a huff, sitting with her back to us. Body language for a cat's displeasure.

"Squeaky, we will come back to you. But we must go on this trip."

As we settled into our airline seats for our trip to the United States, all we could think about was how many adjustments this sweet cat had made since accompanying us to Spain. Will she give up on us? Does she

130

think we've abandoned her? What if something happens to us and we can't come back for her? What will become of her? "Please, God, keep our dear Squeaky safe."

Squeaky tried everything she could think of to escape from the house while we were gone. She managed to get a few dresser drawers open, pulled herself in, and scattered underwear everywhere. She must have crawled on her belly to the back of the drawer where she thought there was an exit, or at least a safe place to hide. She jumped on tall furniture, knocking things over as she looked for a way to escape through the ceiling.

I want OUT of here! I'm scared! Where are Scott and Carolyn? They told me they were coming back!

She tried repeatedly to run out the door each time our neighbors came to feed her. Being locked inside was terrible for her. She must have been so afraid and lonely. Fight or flight, again.

When Scott and I returned to the Lagar, we were very relieved to see Squeaky alive and well. She ran out the door to freedom, barely acknowledging us.

They can just wait. I want to roll in the grass and

breathe some good air.

Our neighbors were upset because they knew Squeaky felt like a prisoner in the house while we were gone. They reprimanded us for not leaving her outside as they had originally requested. They were good-hearted folks, but the Spanish concept of cat-sitting was a little too loose for us. She might have been fine if she'd stayed outside as our neighbors suggested. They would gladly have come to feed her outside every day. But for three weeks? We just couldn't take that risk. We were compelled to protect her. That was our bottom line. Now we realized that until we could find someone whom Squeaky liked as a cat-sitter, we couldn't travel away from the farm together on long trips.

"What about mini-trips away from here, maybe four or five days at a time, sort of like practice sessions to get Squeaky more comfortable with occasional absences? Pretty soon you and I will feel like prisoners here if we can't ever leave for more than a few hours," I complained, worn down by the lack of good options and frustrated because I wished Squeaky would just be a little friendlier with people. I knew that the same people weren't eager to care for Squeaky again, plus they were busy building a new home. Who in the world could we find to penetrate Squeaky's personal security system?

A delightful young couple moved into an old ruin of a lagar very near ours, eager to throw themselves into the long-term manual labor necessary to make it their home. They walked over to visit us often, all of us sharing stories of our lagar restoration woes and triumphs. Scott and I enjoyed the fact that they both spoke perfect English, making conversations effortless for a change. Squeaky would sit on the patio with the four of us on summer nights, seeming to enjoy their company, too. We were thrilled when they offered to care for Squeaky if we ever wanted to get away from the farm for a short trip. We already had a destination in mind!

We'd head for the Atlantic Coast of Spain, to Punta Umbría, to take in the cool maritime air, clear the farm dust out of our lungs, and celebrate our wedding anniversary. We would celebrate coming full circle. Scott and I met in Spain in the mid-1970s and vacationed there often over several decades, after settling down to marriage and careers in the States. Now we were retirees living and working on a farm in Spanish vineyard and olive country. A dream come true, shared with our wonderful Squeaky.

We knew this *simpático* couple would be very conscientious about Squeaky's care. It seemed we'd found a good plan for short trips and if things went well, perhaps it would be an option for future long trips. We discussed Squeaky's care at length with them. They were to feed her in the morning, make sure she always had access to fresh water, let her outside during the day and call her back to the house in the evening. Feed her again and leave her inside until the next morning. We left contact information, the local vet's phone number, lists of reminders for Squeaky's care and a box of Squeaky's favorite toys so they could play. Last, but not least, a little chat just before leaving to let Squeaky know our plans. She watched us pack those dreaded suitcases again, nervously watching our every move.

"You'll get to be an indoor/outdoor kitty this time,

Squeaky. Our friends will spoil you. We love you and we'll miss you. We're going to look for a house to rent next time so you can go, too. We'll be back before you know it."

I thought the three of us would always be together here.

As we headed off on our six-hour drive to the beach, we felt like kids on the way to a candy store. "No worries," said Scott. "What a relief to be able to get away for a few days and know Squeaky doesn't have to spend the whole time locked inside. It's a good time to do this experiment. The weather is nice, not too hot, so she won't get dehydrated when she's outside. She'll be fine."

When we returned from our relaxing mini-vacation, Squeaky seemed in good spirits. Our friends had done everything just as we wanted. They were a little disappointed that Squeaky was aloof. Sometimes she wouldn't come in the first time they called her. Finally, she'd show up, run inside to gobble her food, and rush upstairs to sleep for the night.

Don't follow me, either. I don't want to play with you.

"Just takes some getting used to," we decided, agreeing that the first experience went pretty well, certainly different from the time she had to stay in the house for so long. They offered to be her "sitter" again sometime. Things were looking up.

The young couple cared for Squeaky occasionally for short time periods after that. It was never ideal because Squeaky was always aloof, but at least they were reliable. Squeaky ignored them most of the time, but they still took good, conscientious care of her. Things took a turn for the worse when we went on a longer trip. Squeaky decided to rebel. She refused to come in at night when they called her. They would walk all over the farm in the dark, with a flashlight, trying to coax her to come to the house. *Nope.* She would not cooperate. In fact, our mischievous Squeaky probably had great fun eluding the very people who were trying so diligently to protect her until we came home. She was always near the house in the morning, waiting for her food. They'd try to pet her after feeding her.

Leave me alone. You're not my mom and dad.

She'd bolt down her food and dash back out the door. What if one morning she didn't return? They remembered our stories of how she hated being trapped inside the house a few years before, so they didn't want to lock her inside. But after several nights of exasperating efforts to entice Squeaky back to the house, they decided one morning after breakfast to leave her inside. Better for her to be safe and hating it than to stay outside one time too often.

When we arrived home, they were obviously shaken, quick to let us know Squeaky was a real brat. Squeaky had alienated two more goodhearted people who were trying to make her comfortable in our absence.

"Good grief, what is the matter with Squeaky? Why is she being such a rebel? Now no one wants to take care of our stubborn little friend." I turned to Squeaky. "Where in the world were you? You might have been hurt hiding outside like you did. Why didn't you let our friends take care of you?"

They don't understand me like you do.

"We try so hard to make things work out for you, to keep you safe. Don't you trust us? Did you think we abandoned you?"

No response, but I could imagine what Squeaky was thinking.

Well, I was kind of worried and more than a little mad at you. But, hey, I'm a survivor kitty. I was looking out for myself. Glad you're back, though. Now I can come and go as I please.

Within a few weeks after our return, things were back to normal. Squeaky was outside with us while we worked near the house. We had purchased large rolls of bird netting and were cutting them into pieces suitable for covering the grapevines to protect the grapes from hungry birds. Squeaky came up to me, clearly with a mission. I petted her and talked to her. She wasn't interested.

"Well, fine then. Why did you bother me, Squeaky? You *are* a brat sometimes."

We were outside by the dining room window, near the earth-oven, facing the stone wall. Squeaky gave me one of her mental telepathy looks.

Pay attention, please. Don't drift.

"What do you want me to know, Squeaky?" She darted halfway into the hollowed-out bottom part of the earth-oven, where we kept kindling stacked for fires, turning her head to make sure I saw her.

"Squeaky, don't go in there. It's dirty and buggy; you'll get filthy. Come out, you know I'll never be able to reach you. Please, no hide and seek games right now."

What was she up to? Squeaky crept all the way to the back, behind the kindling and twigs, nestling just out of sight so I had a hard time seeing her. She was probably pretty safe there, hidden from animals and... neighbors who were trying to find her.

"Squeaky! This is where you hid when our friends were looking for you. That's what you're showing me. You were safe even though you were outside at night, but close to the house so you just appeared in the morning to walk through the door for breakfast when they came over. How could you be so mean to them? They wandered all over the farm for hours at night looking for you, calling you, and you didn't come out."

I don't like it when you leave me. If I can't go with you, I'll just take care of myself, thank you very much.

"Oh, Squeaky. You hate it when we leave, don't you? I wish we could always be together. I am so sorry we couldn't take you with us, sorry that you had to hide to feel safe. You sure found a good spot."

I have a lot of hiding places you don't know about. I might have to hide from Peli sometime.

"Come here, please, Squeaky. Thanks for showing me. We're all together again now. Do you know, we miss you so much when we're away? We talk about you all the time."

She came out triumphantly from her hiding place, purring with satisfaction. Dirty, of course. We sat contentedly side-by-side for a while on the little *esparto* (reed) chairs by the stone wall. All was right again in Squeaky's world.

"What a headstrong little girl," I muttered under my breath, as I reached over to pet her. Almost three years after moving to Spain, we were back to Square One as we continued to seek better options for her care when we traveled.

******

One day, on a trip to Cáceres to renew our residency permits, we stopped at a mega-store to get groceries. A large magazine section caught my eye so I started to browse. I was drawn to a Spanish purebred cat magazine. "That's surprising," I thought. "Who would have guessed there would be any interest in cats in this dog-loving society?" I turned to the advertisements in the back, looking for some cat-kenneling options. None for our area, we were painfully aware of that by now, but there were two options in Madrid. "This is wonderful!" I bought the magazine, eager to get home to check out their websites for more information. After all, if we always booked flights to the U.S. out of Madrid, maybe we could take Squeaky along with us and check her into a boarding kennel before we drove ourselves to the airport.

One of the places was in a veterinary office. They had limited kenneling space, used mostly for post-op patients. Their office was in central Madrid, a traffic nightmare during the hours we would need to take Squeaky there. Dogs would be kenneled onsite as well, something we preferred to avoid. The veterinary's staff was familiar with the other place listed in the magazine, and highly recommended it because it was only for cats. *Residencia Felina Alto Nivel, Los Lagos* (Quality Feline

Boarding, Los Lagos). My hopes soared. Scott and I searched the website information for Los Lagos. It looked like a good match for our needs.

"Let's check this out," said Scott. "This time I want to have the information before we plan a trip. We need to know if Los Lagos is a viable option or not."

I phoned the owner, Anabel Vargas, the next day and gave Scott a glowing report. The bonus was that although her kennel was located way on the outskirts of Madrid, it was in the direction of the airport. That meant we could avoid the hassles of Madrid traffic congestion and head toward the airport, getting Squeaky to her "pet hotel" along the way. We would have to meet Anabel and evaluate the kennel.

We drove three and a half hours to meet her and visit the kennel. Squeaky went with us. We wanted to see her reaction to Anabel. The individual cat kennels were clean, large enough to play in, with a soft pillow for napping and stretching, a removable carpet, a litter box, personal bowl of water and food container plus a feather toy to encourage play. Each kennel had a private entrance to a securely enclosed outdoor area where the cats, one at a time, could go to roll in the dirt, feel the sun on their bodies, and connect to the earth. Good news for our *campo* kitty.

Anabel is skilled in basic vet care, able to identify health problems and treat ailing cats, give them meds, and if need be, take them to a veterinarian for more critical care. She grooms the cats often, checks them for any signs of problems. We were lucky to find her. The kind of professional care she offered for cats was quite rare at that time in Spain. Best of all, Anabel and Squeaky seemed to get along.

Anabel had been the President of the Madrid Cat Club and was a great resource and inspiration for an increasing number of city folks becoming interested in cats and how to relate to them. Many Madrileños, because of population density and corresponding satur-ation of living space, were now living in small studio apartments too tiny to accommodate the favored dog. Modern life and progress created a great market for Anabel, who encouraged dog lovers to take interest in cats. "CATS?" was their predictable response. She'd explain that cats are much more adaptable to small living spaces than the large dogs Spaniards prefer. Cats, being naturally clean animals, can be litter-trained and left inside. They are great housemates, and you don't have to walk them every night when you get home from work, or in the morning before work. A large cat can be easier to deal with on a daily basis in small quarters than a small dog. The variety of cat breeds allows a wide range of choices for people seeking animal companionship.

Anabel's favorite specialty breed was Maine Coon cats. She was convinced Squeaky had some Maine Coon characteristics mixed into her multiple blend, pointing out her tufted ear hairs, large paws, long, thick gray-brown fur, and distinctive facial expression.

We sensed Squeaky would be safe at Anabel's kennel when Scott and I went to the States for two to three weeks. Hard for a *campo* cat to be confined, but we knew we couldn't keep leaving her outdoors at the Lagar to avoid the very people who volunteered to feed and care for her while we were away. A few months later, we'd take Squeaky to Los Lagos for her first stay, and Scott and I would catch a flight to the U.S.

We were up before dawn on the day we made the

three-and-a-half hour trip with Squeaky to Los Lagos. First, turn on the generator. We needed electricity to pump water into the cistern, and to provide lights and hot water. Shower, use the hair dryer, chug a quick *café con leche*. Vacuum one more time, pick up all hand tools, buckets, bowls, empty clay pots that were outside and put them in the garage. Empty the trash into plastic bags to drop off at the garbage bin in the pueblo on our way to Madrid. Check the doors and shutters to make sure they are locked. Turn off the generator!

"Did you put all the suitcases in the car?"

"Do we have the key to the front gate? Money?"

I checked my purse again and again for tickets, passports, residency permits, any paperwork we might need to go through Customs as we left Spain and entered the U.S. It was detail overload each time we headed out for a transcontinental trip. After all, we couldn't hurry home to pick up something we had forgotten, with so much distance between Madrid and the farm. Our trip preparations always seemed to leave us feeling awfully out of control. We had spent weeks working double-time to get seasonal farm projects completed before our travels. No farm hands to help out before, during, or after the trip. We couldn't offer full-time employment to anyone, and those who came part-time for special projects came when their schedules permitted, not necessarily when we needed them. The proverbial Buck stopped with us.

"Don't forget Squeaky!"

We put her in the car last, after everything else was packed. She was already nervous, having watched us prepare for the trip. We hadn't let her outside in the morning because she would probably have hidden from us. She felt trapped and was already meowing her discontent when we eased her into the kennel and wedged it between our pieces of luggage on the back seat.

"Squeaky, don't be scared. You don't have to be on a plane. We're going to take you to Los Lagos so you can have a spa vacation while we're away. You remember Anabel, she's a really nice lady. You'll get along fine."

You're driving me crazy! I never know if you're leaving me someplace locked up forever.

When we arrived at Los Lagos, we made sure

Anabel had all the details she might need to know in our absence, including Squeaky's health history, veterinarian phone number, our U.S. phone number in case of emergency, and the date of our return. Finally, we said a reassuring goodbye as we left a nervous Squeaky in Anabel's care.

Hey! Are you coming back? I won't know how to find you.

We phoned Anabel several times from the States to make sure Squeaky was okay. "Yes, she's fine. She went outside to the cat-run today and rolled around in the dirt for a long time. She's eating her meals, drinking water and loves it when I pet her. She's so *linda* (pretty/sweet) and *muy cariñosa* (very affectionate)."

Squeaky seemed fine when we picked her up on our return to Spain. She acted glad to see us, meowing for a while in the car on the way to the farm.

What took you so long? I thought you forgot all about me.

As soon as we were home, we let her out of the kennel and fed her.

"Squeaky, we missed you so much. It's so great to be back at the farm together. We're really proud of you.

Anabel thinks you are a very special cat."

She's okay too. But I don't like being penned up.

She headed off to the fields, so happy to be back. Scott and I smiled at each other, a little lump in our throats as we watched her burst into her free *campo* kitty life again. We were so grateful she had weathered another adventure and returned with us to the farm.

Exhausted after seemingly endless travel, we looked around grimly at all the work to catch up on and realized what comfort we took in having Squeaky with us.

"I'll bet she'll come and snuggle with us tonight."

She stayed outside really late. Scott and I waited up for her.

Chapter 11

Finding Squeaky

Sometimes Squeaky would hide not only from neighbors or scary animals and noises, but from us, too. Especially when she wanted to stay out at night because it was finally cool. Or when the light from the moon and stars was so illuminating and ethereal that she was mesmerized. Or when she zeroed in on a field mouse or gecko, ready to pounce. Day or night, when Squeaky wasn't ready to come in, it was time for the "Find Squeaky" game. She loved to ignore me as I walked around outside the house, calling her.

"Squeaky, please come in. It's after midnight. We're sleepy. You have to come inside to sleep. I know you want to stay out, but it's safer inside. I'll give you a treat, too."

Oh, boy, I love it when the bargaining begins. I don't want food. I'll catch my own if I can stay out tonight, look at all that moonlight. It's a perfect night for hunting. You'll never find me.

"Squeaky, please, we turned the generator off hours ago. It's time to come in. We're tired."

Oh, she drives me crazy. Why can't they just go to bed and leave me out here? Well, I guess if something scares me, I'd rather not be out here alone. What if Peli shows up again? Maybe I'll just wander over to the front door. That's the last door they close at night.

"Oh, thank goodness, there you are! Shame on you for keeping us up so late. Squeaky, hey! Quit trying to get away from me!"

I changed my mind. Let me go!

"I'm holding you tight until we get inside. Say goodnight, Squeaky."

Then there were the times she didn't want to come in the house during the day, whatever the weather, no matter how long I called her.

We didn't want to leave the farm if she was still outdoors somewhere because we never knew when Peli might come back. So, we tried to get her to come in whenever we left. I'd start the search early, but some days there was just no response.

Where the heck was she? We always checked all her favorite hiding spots: on the roof beside the warm chimney, under the car, the cat-sized spaces between logs in the woodpile, under the earth-oven. Nothing. Sometimes she'd show up eventually, irritated that she had to come in.

I'm sick of you calling me to come inside! I just get comfortable somewhere and you decide to leave.

Often, we didn't leave the farm because we couldn't find her.

One sunny, chilly fall day, I went outside to the back of the house to check the water level in the furnace, which provided us with hot water as well as heat. We had lots of gauges to check. We routinely looked for problems before they required major maintenance. Sometimes it would take weeks for repair people to come out to our farm.

Once we had to wait three weeks in cold weather for the repairman to fix the furnace. Another time we waited just as long when the generator failed.

Without the generator, we had no electricity to pump water or start the diesel-fueled furnace. We were left without heat, hot and cold water, and lights at night. We couldn't re-charge our computer or use small appliances. Similar inconveniences occur wherever there is an electrical power outage.

The bright side, though, was that we could still use our refrigerator and stove/oven because they ran on tanks of butane fuel. We had never seen a butane-fueled refrigerator before. They are very expensive, even the mid-sized one we purchased, but sure worth the investment. The butane canister, easily replaced when empty, provides a constant source of alternative energy, eliminating the need for electricity.

We frequently found ourselves frustrated by repairman "no-shows," even after solemn promises of "*No se preocupe, Señora, esta tarde vendré* (Don't worry, Ma'am, I'll be there this afternoon)."

This kind of delay happened frequently, as we

lived off the beaten "repair" trail and it was more cost-efficient for repairmen to work in town. But we often stayed on the farm waiting for them instead of making necessary trips to do errands. It was frustrating to spend so much time being stood up.

Scott's "Handy Andy" practical approach to average mechanical problems was the glue that kept our place functioning. Without his perseverance and logical perspective, we couldn't have survived.

We used to joke that "between the two of us we're a whole person" because Scott needed me to translate the problem to the repairman, but I couldn't understand the response because I'm mechanically challenged. As I struggled to translate into English what the repairman said, Scott would fill in the blanks because he understood mechanical things, so it worked out!

As usual, when either of us was outside, we'd glance around—anything look different? Has a solar panel fallen over in the wind? Any foxes crossing our property looking for food? Squeaky, for example.

I looked over at Scott's tractor, wrapped snuggly in a heavy plastic tarp, not to be used again until spring.

The sun was shining down on it. Scott loved that tractor.

He learned to drive it very carefully over our rocky, hilly terrain. The pueblo folks were sure he'd never be able to drive it without killing himself. They even stood on a hill in the distance watching him practice. How could a city boy from the United States ever learn to drive a tractor in the *campo*?

I was worried about Scott's safety too, but I knew Scott had spent almost every summer of his youth riding around his grandpop's farm in Nebraska on a tractor. At last, Scott had his very own farm and a secondhand Chinese tractor. I think his grandpop would have been proud.

Finally purchasing a tractor helped enormously and eliminated a lot of strain on Scott's deteriorating hip. Now he could keep the farm cultivated and clear of weeds.

We bought a little trailer for the tractor so we could collect prunings, sacks of grapes and olives at harvest times, and to haul debris to the burn pile in the back field near the *era*. We took great pleasure in the blessing of chores made easier.

The tractor didn't fit in our small garage, so it had to be parked outside, covered efficiently to protect it during late fall through winter.

"Uh-oh."

I thought I noticed a bump under the tarp where it covered the tractor seat.

"Probably just a fold in the tarp. It also might be a snake this time of year, seeking shelter and warmth from the sun. Maybe I'll just ignore it."

No. I decided I'd better take a look.

I walked closer, not wanting to lift the perfectly anchored tarp and risk tearing it. But I found one little loose corner, got down on my hands and knees, and looked up toward the tractor seat, a little uneasy about what I'd discover.

Not to worry.

There slept Squeaky.

She must have found the spot where a rock didn't hold the tarp close to the ground, crawled in, and climbed up on the seat.

She had it all. Warmth from the sun. Protection from rain. Safety from larger predator animals (and, she probably thought, from us).

"Squeaky! You are incorrigible. Is this your new hiding place?"

She gave me a half-drowsy, sheepish look and went back to napping. She had figured out yet another way to stay outside and be safe.

Smart kitty.

I can't believe she found me! I'll have to look for a better hiding spot.

160

Chapter 12

Squeaky, The Guard Kitty

In autumn, after grape harvest but before olive harvest, we could sleep in and enjoy lazy mornings. Sunrise was later, so it was often too damp outside to begin our chores when we got up. There was time for that cherished cup of *café con leche*.

We'd get some much-needed rest during autumn. We could unhurriedly enjoy small projects like shelling the almonds and walnuts we had harvested a few months earlier. Our two quince trees were ready for picking—their large, pale yellow fruit was used for making *membrillo* (quince paste/marmalade) to serve with the local artisan goat or sheep's milk cheese. It was challenging to choose the perfect harvesting time for quince. Quince fruit ripens in late fall. Predictably, it rains a lot before the fruit is picked and the quince fall to the ground where they quickly rot. A harvest guessing game every year, like most crops.

Squeaky was a lot more energetic in fall than during the heat of summer. No more shedding gobs of fur to help stay cool, nor hours sprawled, trancelike, under a grapevine's shelter from the sizzling hot sun. In fall, Squeaky's long, thick fur kept her comfortable enough to enjoy some real action.

She eagerly participated whenever Scott and I decided it was time to pick quince fruit. Even on drizzly days, we'd glance over our shoulders to see Squeaky frolicking after us, playfully jumping into little piles of leaves and twigs. Then, when she started getting wet, it was time to climb into the crook of the quince tree so she could supervise from a dry vantage point. She looked like a Halloween poster cat, shrouded in the thick fog of a damp autumn day.

Best of all, for me, autumn was also time to pick green olives for home curing. Usually I would begin between mid-October and the first week of November. Olives for making oil were harvested a little later, when the oil content increased with the ripening process. Of all the things I learned to do at Lagar La Señora, picking green, or slightly *pintado* (beginning to change color) olives to cure was the most rewarding seasonal project. Neighbors explained when to pick them, how to cure them, and how to season them. I loved everything about the process. It was the most natural way to enjoy olives. One of my greatest pleasures was to cure enough olives to last us through the year until the next harvest.

We'd eat them plain, rinsed of excess salt, or I'd season them with wild oregano and herbs from our fields. A healthy, satisfying snack. Scott and I still prefer the tangy herbaceous flavor of home-cured green olives to store-bought, pasteurized, overly-seasoned ones.

One sunny, peaceful October day, we nearly lost Squeaky because of my preoccupation with picking olives. When Squeaky saw me leave the house with my olive bucket in hand, she jumped up from her nap on the sunny porch and followed me along the driveway.

Hey, wait for me. I like to go with you.

163

I was headed for the *manzanilla* olive trees near the front gate and didn't want her to follow me. Scott and I decided we didn't want to tempt fate by working too close to the gate when she was with us. The gate faced the road that led to the pueblo.

"Squeaky, go back to the house. I'm in a hurry."

I'll go for a walk by myself then.

I wanted to get started with my project. The sun would be fading when I finished picking and I'd still have to wash the olives at the outside faucet, a chilly job. I decided to let Squeaky tag along as I walked briskly toward the front gate area.

Squeaky was comfortable on the farm by then, successful in her transition from city life to farm life. She had reclaimed her wild nature. She loved her *campo* adventures, her farm, the freedom to roam. It seemed that back when I found her on the hill hiding from Mama, she had made the decision to stay within the stone walls that lined the perimeter of the seventeen-acre farm. What a blessing, because the "outside room" is a vast space without boundaries to cats.

By the time we arrived at the trees near the front

gate, I could tell Squeaky was feeling a little sassy because I wasn't paying enough attention to her. "Squeaky, I have to start working. We'll play an olive game in a little while." Usually she was eager to get me to play. Not that day. Squeaky abruptly walked over to the stone wall by the long front gate and looked up and down to judge the height. Uncharted territory. She glanced back at me, challenging, poised to jump. I could see determination in her sparkling eyes.

I think I'll get on top of the wall so I can see what's out there. Maybe I can find a new place to hide so I can stay outside whenever I want to.

That got my attention for sure. I said, a little nervously, "Squeaky, stay with me; it's too dangerous for you to go out there." Usually, some logical talk convinced her not to do what she was thinking about. But not now. "Oh, please," I thought, "don't jump on top of that wall and onto the road."

I silently admonished myself for having gone close to the road when she was with me. Then, suddenly, as if she read my mind, Squeaky sprang to the top of the four-foot high wall. She stayed there a few seconds, considering her options, then jumped down and ran across the road to the edge of the blackberry thickets.

"Squeaky! Come back!" I moved closer to the wall so she could see me. I couldn't panic and yell at her or she would crawl into the thicket, out of reach. I spoke casually to her, trying to act unfazed by her challenge. "Squeaky, you don't want to go any farther; you'll get pricked by blackberry thorns. Remember the time you got a thorn stuck in your eyelid?"

She crept along the edge of the thicket, sniffing new scents, then turned to face me. I started to come unglued. If I couldn't convince her to come back, she might wander even farther away, caught up in a new adventure. Squeaky was watching me, listening. Maybe trying to make a choice. I knew if I went through the gate and walked toward her, she'd leap away just to tease me. Even worse, if someone drove up the hill right then, the noise of the car would scare her deeper into the thickets.

I said, as calmly as a trembling woman can, "Squeaky, you're not going to like it out there. It's not safe like it is here with us. Cars come up the road and they could hurt you, and mean animals prowl at night.

Anyway, hurry up, it's almost time for your dinner."

Squeaky didn't move. She stared at me, not sure what to do. I sensed she wished she hadn't gone out there, and that she didn't want me to cross the road to get her. I'd have to play the game her way.

"Okay, I have to keep picking olives. I'll just open the gate so it's easier for you to come back when you're ready." I opened the gate just part of the way so as not to make a big production of it, turned my back and nonchalantly walked away. What a gamble. I was terrified of losing her. Especially if something scared her right then. She was wearing an ID collar, but it might break away if it caught on the brambles. I had to trust that she wanted to come back; she just needed an easy way to do it.

Reminding myself to act unconcerned, I silently pleaded, "Please, Squeaky, listen to me. Don't be stubborn. Come back."

In a few minutes, I saw Squeaky from the corner of my eye, moving toward the gate. I couldn't blow it now. "Hi, sweetie, I'm still working over here." She stopped a minute when she heard my voice, clearly evaluating her options. I listened for cars coming up the road, or unusual noises. So far so good. I kept picking olives. Squeaky paused at the gate. She looked up and down the road, torturing me with her decision-making. Then she walked through the open gate into the olive grove. "Don't rush toward her," I thought. She might change her mind and run back out to the road. "That was some walk you took, Squeaky," I said, still standing by the olive tree.

Well, I wanted to see what was over there, but you said it was almost time for dinner.

Squeaky walked closer to me. And closer. I turned to look at her as she rolled in the dirt to have me rub her belly. I did. Then I picked her up and cradled her in my arms, giving her a back massage as I ran my hands along her spine and sweet-talked her. She's always liked that. Still holding her, I closed the gate.

"Squeaky, our place is here, inside the gate. If you cross the road, you might get lost or hurt and not be able to find us again. We have to stay together." I left my olive bucket by the tree and walked with her in my arms down the driveway toward the house. Halfway home, she squirmed and wanted down. Another rub and roll in the dust. And back to the house for her dinner. To my knowledge, Squeaky never went outside the front gate again.

******

Life wasn't just about olives this time of year. Our To Do list remained active. Intense summer sun and heat had dried out the firewood we purchased every year. Now it was time to cover the pile with tarps to keep the wood nice and dry during winter rains. We used the fireplace daily this time of year for extra heat and for cooking.

Roof tiles that had slipped out of place needed to be re-positioned to prevent leaks. While on the roof checking tiles, Scott would make sure the solar panels were still properly anchored for stability in winter's high winds.

Our winterizing process included ordering diesel fuel for heat, tractor, and generator use. Delivery had to be timed to arrive before heavy rains began. Weather patterns weren't always predictable and the rainy season sometimes soaked the roads before the delivery. The diesel fuel delivery truck driver had a hard time getting up the steep, rocky road from town, even in good weather, but the trip was especially difficult when heavy rains turned the roads slick. Then came an even greater challenge—navigating the curvy hill leading to our diesel holding tank. The driver would speed along our driveway as fast as he could safely maneuver the truck, gaining momentum to climb the slippery hill without getting stuck. We greatly admired the aggressive driving skills and nerves of steel exhibited by the many drivers who delivered fuel to our farm. Scott and I thought of them as stagecoach drivers of the Wild West, expertly driving their coaches and cargo through hazardous terrain. Whenever Squeaky saw one of those big trucks slip-sliding up our driveway, she judiciously ran for cover.

Yikes! Is that an airplane? I'm hiding.

Squeaky developed a morning routine, too, on those lazy fall mornings. First, she had to get us out of bed. She would jump on the bed to wake us, rousing us gently by walking right over to our faces and purring seductively in our ears. We'd usually ignore her, hoping she'd go away and let us sleep some more.

You can't outsmart me. I'll pretend I want to get under the covers.

The next tactic was to poke her head under the covers and act like she wanted us to lift them a little higher so she could navigate her way underneath to snuggle with us. Sometimes this worked, and she'd decide to take a little nap. Usually not. Having woken us enough to lift the covers, she'd dart away!

I love this game. They are so gullible.

"Squeaky, leave us alone," we'd snap, hoping she'd give up. No such luck. Once we made voice contact with her, her tactics intensified. Jumping back on the bed, she'd walk across our pillows, scamper across the blankets, leap over our bodies.

"Please let her get bored and go away," we'd mutter.

Ignoring Squeaky didn't work. Her ace-in-the-hole was to spring from the bed onto the bedside table, noisily batting and thumping framed photos, house keys, ballpoint pens, loose change. She never broke anything, but that usually was enough to get us out of bed. It was as if she were saying that she had dutifully and quietly spent the night inside the house with us and wanted food, and the freedom to be outside. Now.

"All right, Squeaky, enough."

In fall and winter, we usually needed to turn on the generator in the morning right after getting up so we could heat the house. But first to the kitchen to feed our morning-monster feline. She loved charging through those two custom-made cat doors. It was hard to remember how she had coped without them.

Squeaky usually gobbled her food and drank some water before Scott left to turn on the generator. She would scurry to the door just behind Scott as he headed outside. Intuitively, she'd stop abruptly to sniff a minute before she left the porch.

I heard something last night. Let's see what was around and if it's still here. I hope Peli hasn't come back again. I thought he gave up cornering me because Scott and Carolyn always chase him away.

After a few sniffs, Squeaky would turn right, toward the stone wall in front of the house. Scott would turn left, toward the generator shed down the driveway. When Scott returned to the house to make our *café con leche*, Squeaky was usually still sitting in the same spot, surveying the field activity. Mice, voles, small critters.

Now for my after-breakfast bath.

They'd give each other a cursory nod, and if she wasn't too busy with important feline matters like bathing and observing, she would roll over so Scott could rub her belly and sweet-talk her a little bit. Then Squeaky would return to her bathing/observation agenda and Scott would come inside to make our coffee. By then, I had washed and dried Squeaky's food dish and stored it until its next use. No need to tempt mice or bugs by leaving her food dish on the floor. If there were hot coals left in the fireplace from the previous night, I'd cut slices of coarse country bread to toast over the coals for yummy *pan tostado con ajo y aceite de oliva* (grilled country bread rubbed with garlic and slathered with fresh olive oil) for our breakfast. We would sit with our treats at the table in front of the window, watching Squeaky and the dawning of a new day in our little valley. How grateful we were for the pleasure of our quiet moment. Anticipating the enjoyment of such creature comforts when our workload permitted was what kept us going during frenzied, intense times on the farm.

We cherished the days like this, when we could amble through our morning instead of race through it. Squeaky seemed to enjoy the change of pace too, able to find us for a quick snuggle or a spontaneous game like Chase and Catch the … little yarn ball, wine cork, olive, plastic bottle cap, marble, a large round plastic button, a yarn catnip mouse … any number of options from things we'd find or that Diane or loyal friends/fans would send her from the States. Squeaky would signal the beginning of the "game" by following me into the kitchen, meowing to get my attention.

"What do you want, Squeaky?"

Now I've got 'em!

Squeaky would make eye contact with me, then begin a calculated sprint followed by a gallop halfway across the room like a racehorse out of the gate, trying at the same time to get some traction on the hard brick floors. Certainly not as graceful as a racehorse. Maybe like a racehorse trying to run in the mud. But by then we were laughing as she batted her toy of the moment toward us. We'd bat or toss that toy back and forth with Squeaky until we laughed ourselves silly or Squeaky became bored. Cats are easily bored. In that case, my trump card was a long piece of dental floss. I'd dangle the floss in front of her to swat at over the floor, the arm of a chair, pillows. She stretched higher and higher.

Almost got it. One more try.

BAM! Dead floss. Her eyes sparkled.

"Squeaky, you sure know how to have fun and practice your hunting skills at the same time!"

One foggy morning in early fall, our relaxed routine came to a startling halt. Scott left the house to turn on the generator. As soon as it came on, I started grinding coffee beans in our electric grinder for our espressos. Squeaky, as usual, was poised on the stone wall, gazing out at the meadow. Little did we know that Squeaky was on alert. She sensed something different in her morning view. Something unusual in the meadow below the house. It was on the ground, moving and making crying sounds.

Hey! What's that? Better not be one of those mean cats. I thought they were all gone. No, it's not a cat or the shepherd's dog; not that fox that walks through the farm to look at me; not a lamb. Good grief! It looks like a human! Better keep an eye on this.

When Scott came back down the driveway, he approached her as usual to officially greet her outside. "Hey, Squeaky, how's my pretty kitty? See any mice or voles yet?" She focused on the meadow, ignoring him. "Squeaky, you're so serious this morning," Scott said. She paid no attention to him. "Okay, then, I'm going inside to make Mom and me a coffee."

Oh, no! He's leaving! He doesn't even see what I see. I'll have to show him somehow.

Squeaky abruptly darted two feet away as Scott attempted to pet her. She ignored his affection, gazing intently at the meadow. "Jeez, Squeaky. You're really jumpy this morning. What's going on? What are you staring at?"

Scott scanned the immediate scene: pigpen, stone walls, meadow. "Good Lord, what's that?" he gasped as he saw what Squeaky had discovered. Scott saw an old man awkwardly crawling on hands and knees right past the pigpen! "Carolyn, come out here quick! A man is crawling through the meadow!"

Squeaky, sensing her mission was complete, leapt down from the fence and climbed up to her rooftop viewpoint.

There goes my morning routine. Let them deal with it now. This is really weird.

I rushed to the door. Maybe I didn't hear him right. The generator was noisy. "What did you say?"

"Hurry up! There's a man out here crawling through the meadow!"

"What do you mean, there's a man out there crawling through the meadow? It's probably a fallen tree or an animal for Pete's sake. You must be half asleep, Scott," I huffed. Still, I gathered my coat and gloves and ran toward him. What in the world had he seen that looked like a man crawling through the meadow? No one was ever around that early in the morning, let alone a crawling man. Even the shepherd wasn't coming that day to graze his sheep."

Meanwhile, Scott, who was in constant pain now

from hip degeneration, limped closer to the body. It *was* an old man! He spoke haltingly in Spanish, but Scott couldn't understand the man's words. I couldn't make out much either because his words were slurred.

Had he been drinking? Where had he come from? How in the world had he gotten to our meadow? We cautiously approached the man, not sure what to expect. This was chilling. He was old, disoriented, still trying to crawl.

"See if you can get any information from him, Carolyn. I don't know if he can stand up."

I spoke to him in Spanish. "Are you hurt? Can we help you? What has happened? Who are you? Why are you in our field?"

The man looked dazed and responded with unintelligible words each time I asked a question. Probably even more confusing to him was to have been found by strangers who spoke Spanish with a foreign accent.

His hands and arms were bloody. When we tried to help him up, he moaned and groaned and wouldn't cooperate. Did he have a broken bone? Was he bleeding internally? I tried to get his name. Perhaps he had a family somewhere in the area and they were looking for him. What about a telephone number in town? He didn't respond.

"Oh, dear Lord, what can we do to help this man?" No neighbors were around to help us. No 9-1-1 emergency service. No ambulances or local volunteer fire department. Scott couldn't lift the man to his feet; his hip was too weak. I tried to help, thinking the two of us could lift him, but it was still impossible. The ground was slippery with dew. The man was thrashing. We had to let him sink back to the ground. "If we could lift him, we could put him in the car and take him down to the pueblo *Clínica* (government free healthcare clinic)."

"Scott, I'm going to the house to try to call the *Ayuntamiento* (Town Hall). The *guarda rural* (rural policeman) is usually there from late at night until morning. He will know what to do."

I ran to the house and made the call. No answer. It was the crossover time when the *guarda rural* left but the *Ayuntamiento* staff hadn't arrived yet. I had no way of calling the *guarda rural* at his home. I never knew his last name. Nor did I know where he lived in the village, so it would do no good to take the car and look for him while Scott stayed with the injured man.

"I don't believe this," I grumbled as I returned to the scene. My constant efforts to plan for the unexpected had not prepared me for this kind of emergency. Our wounded man continued to bellow and try to stand. Scott kept saying, "No, no," fearing he would hurt himself more in the process. This annoyed the man, who kept struggling to get up! How strange this must have looked to Squeaky, who remained on the rooftop watching the soap opera unfold beneath her.

Desperate, I walked back to the house and phoned the *Clínica* in the village. I had heard they had medical help there twenty-four hours a day. "Let's hope that's 'every' day," I thought. "Please let someone be there."

A nurse answered the phone and I blurted out the story in horrible Spanish. She was confused at first, but once she realized that we were the "foreigners up the hill," she made more of an effort to understand me. Then she said, "Our doctor won't be here today. I'll contact the doctor who's on call. Maybe he can travel here. You'll have to bring the man in your car to the *Clínica*."

I took a deep breath and explained again. "No, we can't bring him to the *Clínica* because we can't lift him to get him into our car. No neighbors are here to help us and he is bleeding. Besides, we don't know if he's seriously injured. We tried to call the *guarda rural* but couldn't reach him. Please, find someone to help this man."

She promised she'd take care of it. *"No se preocupe, Señora, en seguida viene alguien* (Don't worry, Ma'am, someone will come right away)."

A little relieved, but wondering just how long "right away" would be, I returned to the scene. Scott and the old man were both out of sorts by then. Squeaky still watched us from the rooftop. The phone rang again. I bounded back to the house.

Why is she running up and down that hill?

Tired from all the trips back and forth, I complained, "Where's a cell phone when you need one?" We had no cell phone; there was no coverage in our little valley. I reached the house and grabbed the phone. The nurse was calling to say the doctor had arrived and they were coming up right then. I thanked her and told her I'd run down the driveway to open the gate and would meet them there. On the way to the gate, I stopped to turn off the generator. No *café con leche* this morning after all. Might be the least of our worries.

Just as I arrived to open the gate, I was met by a very charming, friendly nurse and an irritable young doctor. He couldn't understand why we didn't bring this man to the *Clínica*. I explained, again. I sensed that patience was not one of his virtues as I struggled to find the correct Spanish words to convey the facts. The doctor seemed frustrated.

"Why didn't you ask a neighbor to help instead of having me drive up here?"

"Because none of the neighbors have arrived from town. They live in the pueblo and come up to spend the day in the country. We are the only permanent people living here. My husband has a weak hip and lacks the strength to lift this man, so we couldn't get him to our car. The man couldn't speak clearly or understand us when we spoke to him in Spanish. I tried to call the *guarda rural* but he wasn't available. So I called the *Clínica* because I was worried the man's condition would soon worsen without help."

"Look Señora," he complained, "I'm not going to drive my brand new car through your gate, down that bumpy driveway. I'll have to leave it here on the main road."

I glanced at his car, and there sat the *guarda rural*. The nurse had located him and he came, as he should have, as a representative of the local police. He recognized me right away and said, *"No se preocupe."* They were there to help.

All of us wondered aloud who this old man was, and what circumstances had led him to our farm.

Since the doctor wouldn't bring his car down our driveway, he had to walk the quarter-mile to the house. He looked city-professional, all spiffy in a beautiful suit, starched shirt, polished shoes, carrying his doctor's bag. He complained every step of the way about how no one should be allowed to live out in the *campo* because no emergency services are available. "It's not my job to come out and tramp through farms, risking damage to my car, getting dirty on the way to try to help someone in this god-awful countryside. Who is he? You don't even know? How did he get here? Who found him, you?"

"No, our cat showed him to us."

The doctor stopped dead in his tracks, glaring at me. "Your CAT?"

I was fuming now. "Yes, our CAT! She saw him first and stared in his direction until we noticed him. Doctor, we're not having a very pleasant morning, either, but of course we want to help. We have no idea who this man is, we've never seen him before. We tried to find out, but he wouldn't answer."

After a little more verbal sparring, the nurse intervened and, walking alongside me, explained how wonderful the doctor had been to come to our farm on such short notice. Of course, he was just a bit out of sorts having to drive all the way to the *campo*, but *"No se preocupe, todo saldrá bien."*

I was ready to scream, but managed to calmly say, "We are wonderful people also. We love the *campo* and work hard to take care of this property. Finding an injured stranger in our field this morning is a very disturbing incident for all of us, but the important thing is to get help for him. I don't particularly care if the doctor gets his fancy clothes dirty."

At this point, the *guarda rural* joined us as we walked toward the house. He asked me to repeat the circumstances of finding this man, listening attentively as I repeated the morning's events. He took no notes, not uncommon in rural areas where memory is emphasized more than the written word. People remember conversations with amazing accuracy.

When we arrived at the meadow, the man was still trying to push Scott out of the way so he could get up. Scott was visibly shaken, as was I, because of our inability to just pick him up and take him to the *Clínica* when we found him. The doctor was exasperated from the fast walk down the lane, the nurse was trying to placate everyone, and the *guarda rural* was intent on finding out who the man was. We tromped over rocks and thistles to get to our mystery man. Then, as we got really close, the *guarda rural* exclaimed, "Ah, Paco, it's you!"

"So that's his name. You know him?" I asked.

"*Sí, por supuesto* (Yes, of course)," he replied. "I know everybody in this area. He's from Madroñera."

Paco looked relieved to hear familiar Spanish, and groaned loudly.

We all rushed to his side, the doctor and nurse and *guarda rural* examining him. He was confused, hardly able to complete a sentence, and still seemed to be in pain. They determined that there were no broken bones, so they hoisted him up onto his feet and half-dragged him up the hill to our car. Just then I caught a glimpse of Squeaky jumping down from her roof perch, slinking inconspicuously toward the front door of the house.

I rushed to open the door; she'd be safe inside. "Way to go, Squeaky! You were such a good warning system for us. Thank you, thank you. I'll be back soon, I think." I was relieved that she had approached the house just at the right moment so we could go to town knowing she was safe inside. She scoped out the perfect place to lounge.

Time for a bath and a long nap.

I quickly went inside to get our passports and

residency cards, just in case we might have to make a police report. The *guarda rural* went with us, talking to Paco all the way. The doctor and nurse returned to the main road to drive back to town in his cherished fancy car.

When we all arrived at the *Clínica*, the whole town was buzzing about the news of the Americanos and the stranger they found in their field. Was he dead or alive? Many approached the car as the *guarda rural* eased Paco out and helped him into the *Clínica*.

"Oh," they said at once. "It's Paco. How did he get all the way up to their farm? He's always wandering off."

The *guarda rural* told us to wait for him. A police report might be necessary, but he'd try to get more information from Paco once the doctor thoroughly examined him. Later, he returned to join us on the sidewalk. It seemed Paco would be okay. Mostly bruises and scratches. The blood had made it look worse.

Apparently, Paco often wandered away from his home in town to go to the *campo*. His relatives hadn't even realized he was gone overnight this time. He had started on his walk from town up the hill in the late afternoon, wandering over the abandoned donkey paths, passing ruins of once-grand houses, and a few deserted little weekender homes. Paco ran out of daylight before he turned to head home. He'd become disoriented, due to his age, but still had a sense of the direction to town. Only he couldn't see anything. No streetlights. No house lights anywhere. We had turned off our lights, the only ones in the area, before going to bed.

The night had turned chilly and foggy. Paco stumbled into a stone wall in the dark, losing his balance and falling into some giant blackberry thickets, scratching his arms, legs, and face terribly. Having lived his whole life in that area, Paco knew he had to cross a big field, ours, to get to the main road (where the doctor would later park), in order to get back to town. But he had to crawl. He couldn't stand up because his leg hurt after falling on the stones. Paco crawled to where Squeaky saw him. He crept on all fours through blackberry brambles, thistles, sheep droppings, past an old well he might have fallen into, up a slippery hill. He made his way around huge olive tree trunks and over rocks. He could do this because he knew the lay of the land, he could feel it. By dawn, he had reached our meadow. If he had been walking upright, Scott would have seen him when he went outside to turn on the generator. As it was, only Squeaky did. Sometimes it's an advantage, being on all fours, having a cat's line of vision.

We thanked the *guarda rural* for coming, for helping us. "We are really glad he will be okay. Goodness, what a frightful morning for everyone."

He said we did all we could but added grimly, "You are very lucky this man didn't die in your field. There would have been a big investigation by the Guardia Civil to find out if you had anything to do with it."

When we finally returned to the Lagar, Squeaky was anxious to go outside and get on with her day. First, we grabbed her and hugged her tight. "Thank you for being our *guarda rural*, Squeaky! We probably wouldn't have noticed that man if you hadn't shown us he was there. It might have been hours before we noticed him. He was old and so exhausted, he could have died. You saved him from dying and saved us from a whole lot of police trouble! You're The Best! Okay," I said, as I put her down, still petting her. "Off to explore your Kingdom. There will be lots of new scents, I'm sure."

She stopped a minute to lick her paw, very proud of herself.

That evening, as we reflected on the incredibly dramatic day we had experienced, we recalled that Squeaky had not only acted like a devoted *guarda rural* that morning, but on other occasions as well. Many times she heard a car coming down our long driveway before we realized it. If she was outside, she'd come running toward the house until she found us, her action alerting us to possible danger. If she was inside with us, she'd growl as loud as a kitty can growl, announcing a strange noise or presence. When Scott had to travel to the U.S. and I was alone on the farm, Squeaky always stayed close to me, whether I was inside or outside. If she perceived a threat, she'd growl loudly and glare in that direction to warn me. Did she feel instinctively that she needed to protect us as she might once have protected her kittens? Without a doubt, we were bonded. *Familia.*

Chapter 13

First Alert

By week's end, the three of us were immersed in our routines once more. Autumn would soon be winter, a great hunting time for Squeaky. Field mice began seeking warmth near the house. She studied their habits so carefully, I think all she had to do was sit in the right spot and watch them come out of hiding. Pounce.

Wow! Another treat to take to Scott and Carolyn.

Many mornings we encountered abundant tokens of her high esteem for us on the doorstep during that time of year. Her keen hunting skills were quite beneficial. No mice resided in our house the whole time we lived there. Even so, we were solemnly aware of the reality of nature's omnipresent pecking order in the *campo*, whether the intended prey might be a mouse, a bird, a lamb, or Squeaky.

Scott and I looked forward to the beginning of olives-for-oil harvest season. Our leisurely pace of life would soon intensify and we would devote our days to the harvest with little time for anything else. A fire would be roaring in the stone fireplace every day, allowing us to leave a *puchero* (clay cooking pot) filled with beans, meats, and sausages to simmer in the embers for hours while we worked outside. When we returned, tired and hungry from harvesting olives, dinner was ready. The original "crock pot" no doubt.

Just as we headed out the door to begin our pre-harvest tasks one morning, Squeaky ran into the house in a panic.

"What's the matter, Squeaky? Aren't you going along with us today as we prepare for olive harvest?" She sped through her cat doors and ran upstairs.

"I wonder what scared her?" Better check it out. She was our guard kitty, after all. I stepped outside toward the stone wall, looked across the property in front and alongside ours. Nothing suspicious. No fox, no roaming dogs, no truck or car coming down the driveway, no man crawling through the field, no Peli! What a blessing we hadn't seen Peli for a while. Maybe it was getting too cold and rainy for him to pester Squeaky. I looked at Scott in confusion.

"Oh, she's always afraid of the wind," he said. "Maybe she's still a little jittery from what happened a week ago with Paco. Anyway, she's safe inside and we have work to do. Let's get going."

Hours later, we headed back to the house after having chosen and prepared the olive trees to be harvested first. We had laid tarps under those trees and secured the tarps with rocks gathered from the field. The tarps would be used to catch olives as they fell when we knocked them with a *vara*, a long, flexible pole that, if used properly, doesn't damage the flesh of the olive or the small, tender branches of the tree.

After placing the tarps, we drove to the pueblo to pick up more large *sacos* (feed sacks) from the farm supply store. These re-usable *sacos* would be filled with olives. While in the pueblo, we purchased *una barra de pan* (baguette/French loaf) to enjoy later in the day with our fireplace stew. On the way out of town, we stopped to say hello to Juan, the chicken man, and buy some delicious golden-yolked eggs laid by his free-roaming hens. He raised five breeds of chickens as well as turkeys, guinea hens, pigeons, and doves. Juan was a kind man and always smiled when he saw us although he didn't understand half of what we said because of our accents. But he understood we loved those chicken eggs, and that's what mattered.

As Scott drove up the bumpy road, I held the recycled egg carton in my lap so our twelve treasures wouldn't break. Eggs were a staple at our house, always handy for a quick *revuelto* (scramble), with *trigueros,* (wild asparagus) from our fields, or with blanched *habas* (fava beans) from my tiny garden.

I was already thinking about olive harvest details and hoped the weather wouldn't be rainy and cold as is often the case. I wondered, too, if this year Squeaky would again playfully help me harvest olives. She loved to join me as I trudged from tree to tree with my neck bucket. A neck bucket is a rubberized, sturdy personal bucket, hung from the neck by a thick cotton strap, dangling just at or a little below the waist. It is flat on the body side, slightly rounded on the opposite side. A great container for collecting olives off low branches. The technique for getting olives into the bucket was described to us by our neighbors as "milking" the olives off the branch right into the bucket, just as one milks the udders of a cow, or a ewe. Squeeze lightly and pull down, squeeze lightly and pull down. Both hands are free for milking the olives because the bucket is suspended from the neck. Fill the bucket and move on to the next tree.

One day the previous year, as I trudged from tree to tree milking the olives into my neck bucket, Squeaky followed me, often climbing into the crook of a tree, her favorite perch. I leaned down to pick up olives that had tumbled to the ground and suddenly several falling olives hit me on the head. That was pretty unusual, because there was no wind. What in the world? I looked up, and there was Squeaky, mid-way up the tree on a limb, batting olives down for me to pick up.

Hey, Carolyn! Want some olives? What a great game.

Our little *lagarera* (female lagar worker) was quite observant. Her playfulness shored me up with the energy to keep working when my neck ached from the weight of the olives. Time to dump the olives into a larger container that would be collected later by Scott and me.

"Okay, little *lagarera*," I coaxed, grateful for her companionship. "Come down and walk with me to the next tree." We played a quick game of Catch the Olive so Squeaky could practice her slam-dunk skills, and headed up the hill together. Squeaky gifted us with lots of simple, wonderful moments like that.

I hoped she would remember to help me again this year.

******

Once back at the farm after a trip to town, more pre-harvest tasks awaited us. We lugged the heavy steel *zaranda* (olive sorter) from its storage place to a site near the driveway by the old donkey path. That would be our first collection point, close to the house and near the car for loading *sacos* of olives. We liked to start harvesting the smaller trees first, until our olive-harvesting muscles woke up for another year's activity. The *zaranda* was too heavy to move all over the farm when we collected olives. We would move it only two or three times during the whole harvest.

Next, I gathered our rubber tubs for collecting large quantities of olives dumped from neck buckets and tarps. I set them near the *zaranda* so they'd be ready when harvest began in a few days, traditionally right after November 1, All Saints' Day.

The terrain was rocky and hilly, and olive trees were interspersed with grapevines, so during harvest we couldn't access the olive trees with trucks or tractors. I'd carry the tubs to the edge of the driveway and Scott would load them and drive to the *zaranda*. We'd hand-sort the harvested olives through the narrow slits of the *zaranda* to remove sticks and stones, leaves and pebbles. The cleaned olives fell into a large tub. When the tub was full, we'd pour the olives into the *sacos*, which held about twenty-five kilos, a little over fifty pounds. Lots of olives would spill to the ground instead of into the *sacos*. Another great opportunity for Squeaky to entice us to play slam-dunk "olive basketball."

We could fit about ten *sacos* at a time in our mini-van. Then we'd drive down to the local olive collection warehouse where the *sacos* were weighed, a record of the weight meticulously kept by the cooperative representative who appeared yearly at harvest time. The *sacos* were emptied of their contents and given back to us. Back to the farm to load more olives, then a return to the warehouse. This routine continued daily, rain or shine, for about two months as we slowly harvested our olives. Luckily for us, olives don't ripen all at once. The few times we were able to hire a work crew from Madroñera to help harvest the olives, we were humbled by how fast and efficiently they worked, compared to how we poked along. But Squeaky never ventured out to "help" them or play Chase the Olive. I think she liked our slower pace; we always had time to notice when she was ready to play.

Olive harvest season spans three or four months, depending on whether fruit production is high or low, and whether the olives are harvested manually or mechanically. Scores of farmers arrived at the olive warehouse daily with their harvested olives. Some were from huge farms and arrived on tractors hauling large trailers filled with olives; others, like us, used their cars or small trucks to transport their bounty. Even a few people arrived with *sacos* slung over a burro. Scott and I always enjoyed the feeling of unity among us all at the end of a long, hard day harvesting olives.

Since the olive mills in Madroñera had been closed for years, semi trucks arrived at the warehouse on an almost-daily basis during harvest season to transport the olives to a large processing mill in another town. Months later, payment would be received by the hard-working farmers who could choose whether they wanted to be paid in olive oil or money.

******

As we walked back to the house after preparing for the

olive harvest that would begin in just a few days, we looked forward to a lazy evening. From now until the end of harvest season, there would be little time to relax. I could tell Scott was looking forward to sitting down, though he didn't say so. He had been stressing his hip all day as we worked.

Just a few hours remained until dark, and the air was getting cold. "Ummm," I purred, "I'll bet the stew is just perfect right now. I'd better get it out of the embers and set the table."

"Let's celebrate this pre-harvest calm before the storm," said Scott. "I'll get a bottle of my wine from the *bodega* and stoke the fire while you serve the stew. And don't forget the baguette!"

I smiled tenderly as I thought about how Squeaky loved to join us after her meal, bathing on her little *esparto* chair in front of the fire while we sat at the table savoring our *campo* food. It was all so blessedly simple. Hard work. Good food and wine. The three of us enjoying a great fire.

"I'm starving," I said. From habit I glanced at the sky on my way into the house.

"Oh, no! Scottie, look at all the buzzards circling over our meadow. What could they be looking for here? We don't have livestock."

Scott looked where I pointed. "They're hovering over the *era*. We'd better check it out." We shared a glance, each thinking, "Darn it, we almost made it into the house without a hitch!"

Suddenly, I froze. "Where's Squeaky?"

I thought she was inside. I prayed she was inside. "Did you let her out before we went to the pueblo?"

"No," Scott quickly reassured me. "She's still inside."

By the time we reached the *era*, the buzzards were feeding. What animal had been so unlucky? How had it died? We were almost afraid to look. As we got closer, the buzzards reluctantly dispersed.

"Can you see what it is?" I asked Scott, hesitant to get close.

"Not yet."

I walked near enough to see a mess of fur, entrails, half-picked bones.

"Oh, God," Scott said softly. "I think it's Peli."

"You're kidding," I stammered. "It can't be him; he's been gone for a long time."

"I know, but get closer so you can see. I think this is a piece of his bobbed tail right here. And look at the color of the fur—gray-blue."

I moved a bit closer to get a better look. It *was* Peli. "This must be what scared Squeaky early this morning. I wonder if he was dead when Squeaky found him? Then the buzzards came."

We both stood there in disbelief. How many times had we wished he would go away and stop persecuting Squeaky? How many times had we felt bitterness toward him for attacking Squeaky that summer day? Now, he was dead. Eviscerated. Reduced to a pile of fur, a piece of a tail, and bloody bones.

All we could feel was remorse for having hated him. And sorrow. Sorrow for the once-strong survivor. Sorrow because his birth circumstance doomed him to a life of rejection, disease, and agonizing death.

"What happened to him?" I wondered aloud. "Scott, he's too pecked at by the buzzards to tell if he was shot by a hunter, or mauled to death by a fox. Did he get caught in an animal trap, escape, but bleed to death?"

"I don't know. Maybe someone on another farm put poisoned food out to kill rats and Peli ate it. And why did he find his way here, to die on top of the *era*?"

Unanswerable questions.

Our yearned-for meal by the fire didn't seem too appealing right then. We stood solemnly in front of the *era* for a few minutes, trying to come to terms with Peli's harsh death. Scott broke the silence.

"Carolyn, I can't leave him here like this. I'll go get a shovel. You find a big plastic garbage bag to hold what's left of him. We'll bury him, deeper than we buried Mama. Maybe he won't be dug up by another animal like she was."

Much later, Scott and I wearily climbed the stairs to the bedroom where Squeaky was dozing on the settee. Our long day had taken its toll on our spirits. We needed to be with our devoted companion, the precious creature we were determined to protect. Seeing Peli torn to pieces had shaken us. Could we continue to keep Squeaky safe from harm?

"Well, Squeaky, how's my kitty?" I sighed as I sat down beside her, petting her. She purred and touched my hand softly with her paw, soothing my spirits with her affectionate gesture. "I guess you already know you won't have to worry about Peli anymore. Now we understand what scared you this morning."

You just noticed? It took you all day!

"You let us know something was wrong this morning but we couldn't figure out what it was. Scott and I didn't find Peli until late this afternoon. He died on the *era*."

Good. Now he can't bother me anymore.

"Squeaky, you must always be on guard outside. We don't want you to end up like Peli. It would break our hearts. I'm glad you ran to the house, to us, when you saw him. We all look out for each other, don't we?"

Sure. We're familia.

I leaned over to stroke her face. She lifted her head to touch her nose to mine, her paw still pressing my hand. "That's really sweet, Squeaky," I said, pleased by her display of affection. Then, she looked me right in the eyes and licked my bangs and my forehead as if I were a kitty in need of mama-to-kitty bonding time. Instantly, I remembered seeing a mama cat with a litter of kittens when I was a young girl. The image that came to mind was a mama cat with her paw authoritatively placed on a kitten while she tenderly licked the fur on the kitten's temples, just above the eyes. I was astonished and humbled by Squeaky's sudden show of feline affection. Were Scott and I her "kittens?" Squeaky's tender behavior had bestowed even greater depth and significance on our connection as *familia*.

Chapter 14

It's A Done Deal

Scott knew hip replacement surgery was inevitable. He still tried everything he could think of to avoid it, dealing with excruciating bone-on-bone pain in order to continue living his dream on the farm. He is one persistent man.

It broke my heart to watch him struggle to keep up with farm chores. After working with such devotion for years to restore the beauty of the farm, Scott was faced with a decision to stay or leave. And just when he had accomplished the hardest part. He never complained, yet his face showed the physical and emotional pain he was suffering.

Before his hip problems intensified, Scott had been the worker bee that kept the farm well-maintained and picturesque. His strength, determination, and Can Do attitude whisked us from one project to another.

I was a good helping hand but unable to work at his level, although I think Bud would have been impressed with the evolution of my *campo* skills. My farm fitness had been curtailed, too, although certainly to a lesser degree than Scott's.

During our last few years there, I cut back on some of my outdoor chores, having succumbed to debilitating allergies to dust, pollen, weeds, and grasses—things impossible to avoid on a farm.

Scott and I often discussed hiring part-time labor to ease the burden, but we knew we wouldn't be happy "managing" laborers on the farm, watching them do the work we couldn't. Our exercise philosophy at Lagar La Señora was simple—we would rather spend the day doing hard labor than working out in a gym.

The thrill of completing difficult chores, pushing our bodies to the limit, and analyzing our successes and failures had become an addiction. How could we stay in shape if we couldn't continue to do farm work?

Friends suggested that we sell the farm and buy a condo in a large Spanish city. Scott could have his surgery and recover there, free from so many farm responsibilities. They assumed we would enjoy the modern conveniences of life again and still be able to live in Spain.

"No," we'd say. "All three of us would go crazy."

How could we enjoy city life after experiencing the deep, close-to-the-earth connection we shared on the farm with Squeaky?

Reality inevitably took its toll after five years. Even Scott's never-fail optimism couldn't remedy the dilemma he faced. One day, he spoke the words I felt in my heart, too. "Carolyn, I just can't keep up with the work any longer." A simple sentence concisely expressed the obvious.

"I know."

Scott looked so sad and vulnerable. We hugged for a long time. He had put so much heart and muscle into caring for Lagar La Señora that it was hard to find comforting words right then.

"I guess we have some hard decisions to make," I finally said. "Let's make plans at the table by the window. The view from there always inspires us."

Each with a lump in our throats, we sat down, speechless. We stared out the window for a while, trying to come to grips with the magnitude of this decision.

Scott spoke first. "I'll have the hip replacement in the U.S. I want to be able to talk to my surgeon in English before and after surgery and during recovery."

I agreed. Oddly, it was a relief. I hadn't looked forward to being the one to translate crucial medical information for major surgery.

"We'll have to sell the farm, then move back to Washington State," Scott added. "At least while we're here we can keep everything presentable for selling. If we go to the States first, the farm will be neglected."

"It's better for Squeaky, too," I replied.

Scott felt the same way. "We can't drag her back and forth with us on those long international flights. It's too tough on her. I think we just need to cut the cord and get on with the three of us returning to the States to live."

Squeaky sat near us on her little *esparto* chair, ears up, purposefully watching us.

I'd better be on guard. Every time they get serious like this, somebody goes on a long trip.

Chapter 15

Foolish Things

Squeaky knew something was up. Realtors and clients visited often, walking through the fields and the house. I cleaned incessantly, always wanting the house to show well. Once an offer of purchase was accepted, we struggled for several months through a bureaucratic maze of paperwork in a foreign language, spending less and less cozy time with Squeaky. We began to pack in anticipation of our departure. Boxes and crates filled the rooms, making Squeaky's access difficult.

What are you doing? This is what happened when we left Seattle. You made a big mess like this in the house. Tell me what's going on!

She'd try her best to lure us into playing one of her favorite games.

I'll chase a wine cork over the floor to get their attention.

"Squeaky, we don't have time to play."

You're no fun anymore.

One evening after I rebuffed her yet again, I noticed the expression on Squeaky's face. Her beautiful eyes searched mine for the truth. "Let's talk, Squeaky."

Uh-oh. She has that serious look.

I sat down, placing Squeaky on my lap. As I petted her, I looked right into her eyes. Squeaky always seems to know when I'm saying something important to her. Did she understand my words, or sense a difference in tone of my voice?

"Squeaky, I'm sorry we've been too distracted to play games. We haven't remembered to tell you how much we love you, either. Oh my, we do love you very, very much. The three of us have to move back to the United States. Scott is in a lot of pain. You've seen him limping. He needs a hip operation. Scott and I can't do all the farm work anymore and there is no one else to help us do it. We're packing our things for the moving company to pick up, just like we did in Seattle. You remember that, don't you?"

Squeaky locked eyes with me but offered no purrs.

"The good news, Squeaky, is that you finally get to go to the beach with us! We've rented a house for a whole month so all three of us can relax and rest up for the big trip to the U.S. in June. Do you know what? We'll have lots of time to play together. I'll be sure to take along your toys and your favorite olive pressing mat for scratching."

Squeaky dug her claws into my knees and jumped off my lap.

I don't want to go anywhere! I like the farm.

I sighed. The weight of our decision to leave the farm was still heavy on my heart. All three of us were discarding favorite things and memories. Scott was in anguish having to leave the hundred-year-old vineyard he had brought back to life and production, vine by vine. The vines returned the favor by yielding excellent fruit and Scott had learned to make very good wine. He has the heart and soul of a grower/vintner and would never be able to replace his experience at Lagar La Señora.

I suspected he would feel the loss of his tractor just as much as I would miss my favorite kitchen of all time, and my cherished olive trees, gnarled and strong. My devotion to olive harvest and yearly home-curing of olives for eating would become nothing more than a memory. And what would spring be without days searching for wild asparagus in our fields with Squeaky tagging along after me, hunting for geckos?

During her six years in Spain, Squeaky had risen to the challenges presented and wholeheartedly adapted to her new life, reclaiming her wild nature. She seemed to melt into the scenery. She became an excellent hunter, an adept observer of her surroundings. She loved her *campo*, her farm, her freedom to roam. Squeaky was still our sweet, gentle All-The-Way-From-Seattle Kitty, though now she was a bit arthritic and tattered. I guess we all were.

At last, the sale of the farm was complete. Squeaky was a nervous wreck, watching yet another drama unfold before her eyes, but not understanding it.

Our small shipment of household goods, which had been transported to Lisbon began its ocean voyage to

Seattle. The only things remaining were those we would pack in our luggage to take with us on the plane, and Squeaky's kennel. We rented a car for the rest of our Spanish travel days, having sold our personal car to a neighbor. Now, the hardest part—leaving.

First, we had to say good-bye to Lagar La Señora. On departure day, we ceremoniously walked with Squeaky in our arms through the vineyard and olive groves, up and down the hills on either side of the driveway. We passed the old donkey path and stood on top of the *era* one last time to see the view.

Tears filled our eyes as memory after memory of our six years of adventures flooded back to us. "Squeaky, look. There's your favorite olive tree for climbing. Near the big grapevine you sat under in summer to snooze. I know you'll miss the stone walls with hidden treasures like mice and geckos. You learned to be such a good *campo* kitty. We are so proud of you! Now we're going on another journey together."

We're coming back here, right?

We positioned Squeaky's kennel and litter box in the back seat of the car, crammed between suitcases and packing boxes. Then we headed to the beach, to our small, furnished rental house almost seven hours from the farm.

Time to relax, to distance ourselves from the arduous process of organizing our return to the U.S. We hoped our time at the beach with Squeaky would revive her spirits.

It didn't work out that way.

Squeaky just couldn't understand why we weren't at the farm anymore. Though she took comfort in our presence at the beach house, she was frazzled, scared, disoriented. She wasn't used to being confined in the house all day and night. Even worse, it was May, very hot, and we couldn't leave the windows open for fresh air because there were no screens to keep her from jumping out.

Where are we? Where's the farm? Why can't I go outside?

She wanted out, and I'm sure if she had escaped, she would have tried to find the farm again. I was terrified that after all the years of protecting her on the farm, Squeaky would slip out the door or a window one day and disappear forever.

Bored by our attempts to distract her with cat toys, Squeaky walked incessantly to the door to let us know she wanted to go outside. I wondered if she thought the farm was on the other side of the door. Her discontentment saddened us, but there was no turning back.

At lunchtime one day, I glanced across the room at Squeaky as I set the table. She was sitting on the olive-pressing mat, her favorite scratching pad at the farm. It had been kept on the side porch at Lagar La Señora for her exclusive use. She loved to scratch her claws over it after a hard day's adventuring, just before coming inside to bathe and nap. It was hers to scratch whenever the urge struck—no scolding by me to leave it alone. Now, the mat was a frayed, worn security blanket. Something from the farm with her scent on it.

Squeaky was leaning against the plastic jug of olives I had brought with us. She liked to lean her head against something. These were the last olives I had cured on our property, to be enjoyed while we were at this temporary beach retreat. The uneaten ones would be thrown away before we returned to the States.

The other object on the mat was an insulated

cooler that held the fresh fish I would prepare for our lunch. It was of no interest to Squeaky. Resignation showed on her face. We were losing our connection. I rushed to her, petting her, trying to soothe her. She ran away.

Don't talk to me! Just take me back to the farm!

I could see Squeaky retreating emotionally. Her vacant expression haunted me, confirming she couldn't understand anything about her life now. An extra glass of wine with lunch that day took me out of my head and into my heart. I let go of all the endless details involved in getting us back to the U.S. and looked for my special friend, who was... under the bed now. It hurt to see her miserable, imprisoned, unable to be a *campo* kitty. I knew Squeaky tolerated all this upheaval because of our bond. Yet she couldn't understand where we were or why we had plopped her down in a strange place, in isolation.

Why do you make me stay inside? Where am I? What's wrong with everybody?

I had tried to soothe her by reminding her that we had to leave the farm and return to the States to live. I told her we could never have left her on the farm, as many people there suggested. "Leave her here, she's used to the farm. She's just a cat. She'll get along without you."

"Never, not ever, will we abandon you, Squeaky." I'd repeated reassuringly, "We're family. We belong together."

Somehow, I had to get her outside. She would be terrified if I used a leash and harness because our rental house was on a busy street with lots of noisy traffic and sidewalks filled with pedestrians.

What could I do? Reason and logic ceded to matters of the heart. I pulled her out from under the bed, made sure her ID collar was snug, maneuvered her gently into her kennel on a clean towel for traction, and double-checked to make sure the kennel door was properly locked. Squeaky looked worried.

Now what?

I looked at her terrified face and announced, "Squeaky, we are going to the beach!"

Squeaky had no idea what was happening. She huddled in the back of the kennel, those expressive eyes searching mine for the truth.

I spoke firmly to her. "It's simple. I want to show you where we are, that's all. Just another little adventure with my kitty. You'll be safe in the kennel and get to see something you've never seen before—the ocean. Don't worry, I'll protect you."

I let Scott know where we were going. He rolled his

eyes. "Okay, but be careful." He would have gone with us in a heartbeat. But by then he couldn't even walk a block without agonizing pain. Squeaky and I headed off for the six-block walk to the beach. She meowed, faintly.

Where are you taking me? What are you doing?

Poor thing, Squeaky was ramrodded into yet another situation where she'd have to totally trust me.

I walked over rocky paths to the beach, assuring her all the way that she was okay. When we got to the crowded beach, I spread a big towel on the sand, put her kennel on it, faced it toward the ocean and sat down beside her.

Squeaky definitely didn't relax into the moment. She cowered in the back of the kennel.

I leaned toward the kennel door and said, "Squeaky, this is the ocean. I know you are scared. You don't have to leave the kennel. We will go back to the house together. But I wanted you to see and smell where we are."

Spaniards nearby were uncharacteristically quiet as they watched me maneuver the kennel onto the sand and sit down beside it, talking to "something." A few approached to see what was in the kennel. "Oh! It's a CAT!" (Not a dog, an obvious disappointment.)

"¡Qué linda (How pretty)!"

"Is she afraid?"

"Yes."

"Does she like the beach?"

"It's too soon to know."

We were there perhaps twenty minutes. A lifetime of uncertainty for Squeaky, no doubt. Her view was miniscule, framed by the confines of her small kennel. She saw the ocean, heard the waves roll to shore. She felt the wind, the warmth of the sun.

I think I'll just move up a little closer to the front so I can see better.

I noticed her ears were pointed straight up, moving almost imperceptibly to hear every little change in sound, on alert for locator clues. Not a meow or purr out of her, totally fixated on these wild surroundings.

I pushed my finger through a hole in the kennel door and touched her cold, wet nose. She glanced at me, her eyes all sparkly again. Mission accomplished.

"Are you ready to go home now, Squeaky?"

We made it safely back to the house. She cautiously crept out of the kennel and made a beeline for the bedroom to hide under the bed.

You're not grabbing me again!

Squeaky hasn't seen an ocean since then and it may not happen again in her lifetime. If it does, will she remember the beach in Spain?

Scott was relieved we had returned safely from our outing. I was probably foolish to have trudged off with her that day. All logic would have said, "No, leave well enough alone. What if I fall or the kennel door flies open and Squeaky escapes?"

But we had such a strong connection that I sensed her feelings of isolation and confusion.

I understood how it must feel for her to be locked up in that rental house after six years of freedom on a farm. I knew a lengthy journey was ahead as we returned to the States, so I made a decision to show her something new to get her out of her funk.

It was a big chance to take. One of those times when you are keenly aware that things might go well or might end in disaster. You try to get the odds in your favor, but it's a roll of the dice.

Thankfully, it was a safe experience for Squeaky. She didn't stay under the bed for long, but I could tell she was greatly relieved to return home. Now the rental house seemed a better place than the wild, windy beach!

That beach adventure was easy, compared to the turmoil our dear Squeaky would soon face. She would have to travel again, on a seemingly endless trip as we made our way back to the United States.

We planned to begin our journey with a seven-hour drive to Trujillo, where we'd spend the night in a hotel. The next morning our destination would be a hotel in Madrid, near the airport. From there, back to the U.S.

After making the tiresome trip to Trujillo with Squeaky in her kennel, we rattled her nerves even more by sneaking her into the hotel because pets weren't allowed. "Squeaky, please, please, please, don't meow," I begged as I pulled her from her kennel in the car and stuffed her into an empty suitcase. "We can't stay at the hotel if they hear you."

Scott checked us in at the front desk and returned

to the car with the room key. He grabbed some other suitcases as I carried the suitcase with Squeaky inside. "Oh, please, Squeaky, don't make a sound."

One flight of stairs never seemed so long. Squeaky was absolutely horrified. She didn't even whimper. The human she trusted had thrust her into a "box" and zipped it closed! What must she have thought I was doing to her?

As soon as I closed the door to the room, I rescued her from the suitcase and hugged her. I whispered, "Thank you, Squeaky. You did just the right thing."

I tried to pet her but she was frightened.

I prepared her litter box and hastily set some food and water on the floor. Under the bed she went. Right in the middle, just out of my reach. I sat on the floor by the bed, trying to soothe her by explaining why we had to sneak her into the room.

"Squeaky, I'm really sorry I put my sweet kitty inside a suitcase to get her to the room. You were very wise not to meow. If the hotel staff heard you, we would all have been asked to leave the hotel. There are no boarding kennels nearby for cats. In order for us to stay together, I had to take a chance on sneaking you into the hotel."

She scooted even farther under the bed, wanting only to be invisible.

"Okay, Squeaky. Hang in there. At least we're together. You can take a little nap."

Squeaky would make one more suitcase trip.

The next morning, we put her in the suitcase again to get her back to the car. I smuggled her out while Scott distracted the concierge with a tourist question.

Squeaky would spend the next three hours in her kennel while Scott drove us to Madrid, to … another hotel. Thankfully, I'd found a hotel where cats were permitted in the rooms, freeing us from having to sneak her onto the premises.

But Squeaky was irreversibly nervous by now. Spooked. She hid under the bed all night, worrying us with her moaning meows. This time she didn't seek the solace of closeness with us in bed. How much stress could this poor creature handle? Had we pushed her over the brink of trusting us? None of us slept.

At four o'clock the next morning, we fed Squeaky

and gave her water to drink.

She scratched around in her litter box a moment or two, then dashed back under the bed.

Please don't grab me and take me anywhere else. Just leave me alone!

We pulled Squeaky out from under the bed, trying to explain what was going on as we pushed her into the kennel. Lastly, I washed and dried the litter box and packed it into our carry-on suitcase. We would need it for Squeaky upon arrival in the U.S.

We checked out of the hotel, loaded her into the rental car one more time, and drove to the cargo section of Madrid's Barajas International Airport.

Pets traveling on international flights at that time had to be delivered to the cargo section of the airport one hour or more before passenger check-in at the main terminal.

Since passenger check-in for international flights was two hours ahead of flight time, it would be three hours before Squeaky could be boarded.

We would travel to Seattle via London, the exact reverse of the route we had taken years ago on our way to Spain from Seattle.

We left Squeaky in her kennel with the lone, sleepy person in charge of accepting animals for international flights.

The hangar was chilly, windy, noisy. I gave the man the required paperwork, repeatedly shouting travel instructions in Spanish. I showed him our tickets, Squeaky's reservation confirmation, and verified our flight arrangements. Scott and I were her only link. If we failed to check all details and ensure her safe travel, we might never see her again.

"My husband and I must go to the main terminal and can't come back here to check on her. Please assure me you will put her on the plane. Will you remember she's here? She'll be scared of all the noises. Will you be the one who will put her on the plane? If the flight is delayed, where will she be sent?"

On and on I questioned this sleepy man who seemed unaccustomed to answering so many questions about animal care.

Finally he looked me in the eye and said, slowly, *"No se preocupe, Señora, puede usted contar conmigo, todo saldrá bien* (Don't worry Ma'am, you can count on me, everything will be fine)."

I had tried to anticipate all the details for Squeaky's safety during the flight. Now I could only trust that, indeed, everything would be fine.

I spoke to Squeaky often as she sat huddled in the back of her kennel, staring back at me with pleading, frightened eyes. I kept telling her how much we loved her and that we all would be together again soon.

"Don't worry, Squeaky. Everything will be fine. I have to trust the Air Cargo man, and you have to trust me."

Scott, always her calm buddy, spoke firmly and tenderly to her. "Aw, Squeaky, you just take a nice long nap when you get on the plane and we'll see you when you wake up." He looked at me, adding softly, "Too bad the same flight attendants who checked her in for the flight from Seattle six years ago aren't here today."

Squeaky was frantic.

For her, it was like having your second wisdom tooth extracted. Now you know what it's like, and it wasn't pleasant the first time. She had endured one international airline trip. The noises of plane engines, the take-offs and landings, the luggage trolleys, all were painfully familiar to her. She pawed frantically at the door of her kennel, struggling to be free.

Oh, no, don't leave me! Don't put me on a plane again!

I believe panic set in, for Squeaky and for us. Would Squeaky, now six years older, be able to survive another grueling airline flight?

Were we pushing her beyond her physical endurance?

236

Chapter 16

Full Circle

Our spirits were low as we stood in line at the airline check-in counter after leaving Squeaky at the Air Cargo terminal and returning our rental car. We were groggy from not having slept a wink while listening to Squeaky meow all night at the hotel. Non-stop worrying about her well-being on her second international flight kept us jittery.

"It's worse for her than it is for us," I said, as we waited for our turn to check in. "At least we know where we're going and we can move around. Squeaky is trapped in a kennel and feels helpless."

Scott agreed. "I know it's rough on her, but she'll

pull through. She wants to be with us as much as we want to be with her."

The emotional impact of feeling between worlds weighed heavily on us. We looked forward to getting settled in Washington State again, but we knew daily life would never be as related to the earth and elements as it had been in Spain. And how would Squeaky adjust to life in a small yard after roaming seventeen acres for over six years?

First, we all had to arrive safely in Seattle.

Before leaving Spain, I had called the U.S. Embassy to ask them what, if any, paperwork was required to bring Squeaky back to the States with us. They suggested I call the U.S. Department of Agriculture.

The first person I spoke with there said, "If she went over to Spain with you, she can come back with you. No problem. No paperwork required for your cat."

A few weeks later, I began worrying that the explanation seemed too simple, so I called again and spoke with another person. She said the same thing, but added, "Well, if you're concerned, bring a list of her recent vaccinations." Our Spanish vet provided a history of Squeaky's vaccinations for us, which I put in a folder with the Seattle health records we had brought with us to Spain years ago. Just in case.

After clearing Customs in Seattle, I was paged over the loudspeaker to go to the U.S. Department of Agriculture office located upstairs. I climbed the stairs as fast as I could after such a long trip, worrying all the way about Squeaky's welfare. The man behind the desk spoke gruffly. "Where's the paperwork for this animal? We can't let your cat into the country without paperwork. She'll have to be held in Quarantine until we get it."

My heart raced. I told him my experience with the phone calls. He replied that I had received incorrect information. Too bad, but they needed paperwork.

I pulled out my file and handed it to him. "I brought this along just in case. I hope it's what you need."

"Well, it's in Spanish, not English," he retaliated. "We need an official translation."

"I don't have an official translation. I was told I didn't even need paperwork. But I can translate the

Spanish records for you right now."

He reluctantly let me do so and read the Seattle health records too. He handed me the file. "Okay, pick up your cat at Will-Call luggage center."

We headed right to Squeaky, who was sitting in her kennel on top of a counter with a very nice attendant keeping her company.

"Squeaky, Squeaky, here we are! You made it! You are the bravest kitty in the world!" She looked at me with relief and meowed shrilly.

I didn't know where you were. Don't do this to me again!

As I said a silent prayer of thanks for Squeaky's safe arrival, I turned to hug Scott. "We made it back. All three of us are together again." My voice was quivering. "But, no more international airline travel for Squeaky. She's been lucky twice; that's enough tempting of Fate. What if I hadn't brought her health records with me?"

We packed ourselves into another rental car for the short trip to a hotel for a few days. They accepted pets. Squeaky used her portable litter box and headed right under the bed. She spent most of her hotel time hidden under there, until we put her in the car again for a five-hour trip to Walla Walla, our new hometown in Eastern Washington's wine country.

We all felt like vagabonds since leaving the beach in Spain. But at least we would be able to settle into a house soon after arrival in Walla Walla.

We had the good fortune, just before leaving Spain, of being accepted as summer house-sitters for a family in College Place, adjacent to Walla Walla. That lucky opportunity was due to a longtime friend, Dorothea, who referred us to a friend of hers, Verlynn, who lived in College Place. Verlynn referred us to her neighbors, David Cowles and his family. What a wonderful gift of helping hands. Dorothea had started the ball rolling at a really crucial time.

The Cowles family was taking their dog and two cats with them on vacation. Scott and I would tend the house, the aquarium, and their parakeet until they returned.

We were eager to have focused time again with Squeaky, to calm her after so much travel. David and Linda Cowles are lovers of all creatures and were sympathetic to Squeaky's travel saga. They went out of their way to facilitate Squeaky's transition, and ours, from a rural farm to a three-month stay in their house. Scott and I remain thankful to this day for their kindness and compassion toward three strays from Spain.

I explained our plans to Squeaky about our new life in Walla Walla. "Squeaky, I promise you we'll stay in Walla Walla for a long time. You'll like it there. We thought about returning to Seattle to live, but after being on our Spanish farm for six years, we wanted to live in a small community again, in an agricultural area. Scott's friend, John, went to college in Walla Walla and recommended it as a great town. Plus, there are a lot of vineyards in the area so it might look a little like our farm to you. We did lots of investigating and I think you'll like it, too. We are house-sitting for three months and you get to be with us in one place for a good rest."

Can I go outside there?

But first, we had to stay in a hotel for three days waiting for the Cowles to leave on their vacation.

I pleaded with Squeaky as she hid under the hotel bed, "Oh, sweetie, don't worry. You just have to trust me. Everything will work out fine."

I laughed at my phrasing. Now I was using a version of the sentence I had tired of hearing from Spaniards. I imagined Squeaky, too, was no longer soothed by my attempts to reassure her.

"Cheer up, Squeaky, the worst is over. You can relax now."

She didn't.

Maybe she sensed the rest of the story. I decided not to tell her that while we were house-sitting, she would have to be an indoor kitty for three months. That was rough on her and on us.

During those three months, we were able to get a much-needed check-up for Squeaky at a local veterinary office. She was healthy and a hit with the staff because of her unique travel adventures. But she had periodontal disease in a few places and several teeth would have to be extracted. We decided to let her adjust to a new life before having the teeth removed. I felt responsible.

The Spanish veterinarian had insisted that *cats* didn't need their teeth cleaned. He hadn't had the instruments to clean cats' teeth, anyway, so it had been useless trying to convince him it was necessary. Now

Squeaky faced the consequence.

"Well," Scott rationalized, "maybe the bright side is that Squeaky never had to undergo general anesthesia for dental care or anything else the whole six years we were there."

By the time our house-sitting job came to an end, we had purchased a house in Walla Walla with a good-sized yard. Not big compared to Squeaky's seventeen-acre "yard" in Spain. But the house was comfortable and refreshingly functional. Even electricity! Easy living again.

The day we moved into our new home, I lifted Squeaky in my arms and walked through the house with her.

"Squeaky, now, finally, I can say for sure, You are home! We'll all be so happy to have a routine life again. No more airplanes, no more hotels, no more suitcases, no more hours traveling in the car in your kennel. In a few weeks, we'll get our household shipment from Spain and you'll have lots of familiar scents to sniff. Don't give up on us, sweet Squeaky. Things will be better from now on." She looked at me skeptically. I could see she was having a hard time trusting what I said.

Will I be able to go outside again, ever?

I could only hope that adjusting to a new, lasting routine and being free to go outdoors again would lift her spirits.

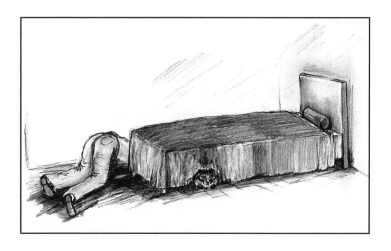

Chapter 17

Get The Leash

We followed our routine for acquainting Squeaky with a new home: keep her inside for a week or so until she was used to the house and the world outside the windows. Then, get the leash and harness and go for a walk.

Is that the leash? Are we going outside?

As usual, Squeaky was eager to get out of the house. It didn't take much time to walk with Squeaky around our small property, but she still scrutinized everything she encountered. Sniff, sniff, sniff. Finding her way again. She knew the drill, and in a very short time adjusted to going outside by herself.

Life was easier and more predictable for us all, but it didn't take Squeaky much time to get bored.

I'll figure a way to jump over this chain link fence. Maybe somehow I can find my way back to the farm. They can't make me stay in such a small yard. The trees are too big to climb; I can't even see the top of them. There's nothing to sit on but the ground. I like the grass, it's soft, but where are the stone walls for me to sit on? I can't see where I am from down here. I checked over and over, and there's no way to get up on the roof to see the view.

Squeaky still liked joining us in the outside "room." She would walk around the yard with us as we discussed plans to use the abandoned garden area to plant a few olive trees for me, and a hobby vineyard for Scott. That would give us a chance to rekindle our fond memories of the farm. Olive trees were a risk to plant in Eastern Washington's climate, but worth a try because I knew how much I would miss gathering and curing raw olives for eating. Scott was eager to learn how to grow and tend young grapevines, but he would have to wait to plant the vines until after his hip surgery.

There wasn't much for Squeaky to do, however.

Yes, there were birds, but only way high up in trees. No foxes, no sheep, no shepherd, no familiar things. She found a mouse one day and made a big deal of catching it and bringing it to us, dropping it at our doorstep.

That was fun! I'm still a good mouser!

But mostly Squeaky would walk listlessly around the yard, then flop down on the grass looking very discontent. No happy eyes.

I'm going crazy. What am I supposed to do here?

Scott and I felt sort of disconnected too. We loved our return to modern conveniences but missed our rustic farm lifestyle.

As I watched our little kindred spirit walking around the yard one summer day, a message came through loud and clear. The Blue Water Bucket.

"She doesn't have a water bucket outside anymore. It's worth a try," I thought. "Maybe I can perk her up a bit."

I went to the store and bought a small blue plastic bucket with a handle, just like the one we had in Spain. I couldn't wait to get back to the house to try the experiment.

"Squeaky, Squeaky! Come here! I have a surprise for you!"

What's that she has in her hand?

I stopped and filled the bucket with cool water from the outside faucet and moved it to a shady spot under one of the tall black locust trees, not far from Squeaky. "Look, Squeaky, here's your own special water bucket, just like in Spain." She pretended not to notice, just like in Spain!

I'll check it out later.

I turned and walked away, amused by her stubbornness. "She wants to find it without my help," I thought.

Sure enough, I glanced back in her direction and there she was, front paws gripping the top of the bucket, hind legs balancing as she drank water, and drank water, and drank water. My spirit soared, seeing her re-live something familiar and "all hers." When she finished drinking, she turned to look at me with a very contented expression.

"I love you too, Squeaky."

A few weeks later, our shipment of household

goods arrived from Spain. Some small furniture, lots of artisan woven baskets, our fireplace cookery, Spanish regional recipe books, and Squeaky's two *esparto* fireplace chairs. Scott and I felt a tug at our heartstrings as we looked at these treasured items that until just recently had been part of our daily lives in Spain.

"I'm so glad you thought to bring those chairs, Scott. Let's put them on the porch and see if Squeaky notices them."

Squeaky did a double take when she walked past the porch.

I just got a whiff of something familiar. Better get closer.

She approached the chairs with suspicion. Slowly she moved closer, sniffing all the legs, then stretching up to sniff the *esparto* seats.

These are my chairs!

In a split second, she jumped onto one, sat down and started bathing. Did she know how long it had been since she had seen the chairs? Had she forgotten about them until that moment? It didn't matter. Seeing her so content was all the proof we needed that she had rediscovered one of her creature comforts from Spain.

She still sits on those chairs on the porch, or by the fireplace with Scott when he builds a roaring fire. He draws up the other little chair and sits next to her, petting her. For a little while, they can pretend they are at the farm again. She also sits on one of the chairs on the porch when Scott and I are watching television. She is jealous of the television and refuses to sit on the sofa with us while we watch a favorite program.

Just let me outside where there's peace and quiet. I'll go sit by myself.

We didn't have a television when we lived in Spain, so Squeaky wasn't used to such competition.

Life back in the United States just wasn't very stimulating for Squeaky. She would play the "chase" games with me in the house, but without much enthusiasm.

I don't want to play with feather dusters and silly cat toys. Why can't I go back to the farm where I can play with geckos and hunt real things?

"Poor Squeaky," I'd say. "I know it's hard for you. We miss it, too. Every day was a new adventure there, wasn't it? But at least we're together and Scott will be able to have hip surgery soon. Then you two can walk around together again in a vineyard. You'll see, things are getting back to normal for us all."

Not long after that, I tracked down a source for fresh, uncured green olives in California. I was so excited when our shipment arrived. The quality was pretty good. Only twenty pounds or so, a whole lot less than the normal amounts I harvested in Spain. Once I sorted and culled out the bruised olives, then rinsed them, I put them right into brine in sterilized containers to "cure" for a year. Now I could cure olives for eating again. Finding a U.S. source helped me nurture a memory from our farm.

I was about to throw out the culled olives when I wondered, "Would Squeaky still play Chase the Olive?"

"Scott, come here; I'm going to see if Squeaky remembers her favorite game."

Squeaky was very, very busy napping on the soft swivel chair when I walked into the living room with an olive in my hand. I held it under her nose. She woke up right away and jumped down onto the linoleum floor. "Squeaky, let's play Chase the Olive!"

I tossed the olive on the floor so it would roll fast. She chased it around the room, under chairs, batting it... finally... back to me! Over and over. We spent a good five minutes frolicking, laughing (well, I was laughing), reviving that fading memory as Squeaky raced, slip-sliding around corners on the waxed linoleum floor, batting the olive. What a precious scene! Scott and I laughed so hard we had tears in our eyes. Squeaky's eyes were bright and alert. Then, in true cat fashion, Squeaky got bored and quit playing the game. Back to the swivel chair.

Now, that's a real toy. Just like at the farm. Time for a bath and a nap.

Squeaky's playful, wild abandon created yet another special moment in our lives. For an instant, we three were back on the farm together. I picked her up and held her close. Squeaky purred her contentment.

"Thanks, Squeaky. We'll always remember our lives together in the *campo*, won't we? *Familia*."

Epilogue

Squeaky, do you feel like a tired old adventurer? We do. Memories of our many incredible experiences in Spain flood through our minds at the oddest times, reminding us again of our deep attachment to the farm and to you. You were re-born there, connecting to your primal instincts. We loved our shared relationship to the earth and seasons.

Back in the United States now, life is safer, more predictable. Not too exciting for a kitty who walked on the wild side. You yearn for us all to be together outdoors like we were at the farm. That hasn't often been the case. Scott and I spend more time in the "inside" room now. You miss space to roam, stone walls to climb, indulgent dust baths on lazy walks down the long dirt driveway with Scott and me. The five hundred olive tree trunks you once used as scratching posts have been replaced with a silly carpeted post hardly fit for sharpening a *campo* kitty's claws. Do you yearn for those glorious nights when you perched high on the tile roof, innately in harmony with the cosmic display of shooting stars and heavenly energy? Where, you wonder, are all those beautiful stars now?

As we bustle around with our distractions and busyness here in Walla Walla, you sit dejectedly on the porch on the little *esparto* chair we brought back for you from Spain. The one from the porch where you used to curl up for a nap in cold weather, or where you sat catching a cool summer breeze. You remind us we were usually sitting with you then.

Our hearts overflow with the love that binds us to you. You rescued us emotionally more often than we rescued you physically, sensing the important, serious times and also the times for a little comic relief. We three became a strong family at Lagar La Señora, each member using our unique skills for the betterment of the whole. What a perfect example you are of "showing," not "telling." When you tire of our self-absorbed urban lives, you retreat, find a quiet spot, and show us again that you know best.

You know The Answer. It's your path to show us. And our path to notice. *Familia.*

THE END

Acknowledgements

The writing of, and illustrations for *Squeaky's Farm* came about because two very talented animal-loving women stepped into my life—about eight years apart. Each one enthusiastically contributed time and talent so that net proceeds from book sales could be donated to animal shelters and feral cat trap/neuter/return programs. Their dedication to that cause shifted the book from concept to manuscript and fueled my determination to complete *Squeaky's Farm*.

What a heart-warming project this has been. If the animals in my life have taught me about devotion, I'd say the humans involved with the creation of this book did the same. Some of the people acknowledged here were directly involved with the production of the book; others were supportive family members, friends, and animal lovers. All shared enthusiasm for learning more about our Spanish adventure with Squeaky. We are very grateful to you all.

Bronwyn Holmes's graphite illustrations beautifully depict Squeaky's adventures and misadventures at Lagar La Señora.

We met in Spain, each beginning a new life in a different pueblo, but sharing a great love for cats. Bron's understanding of felines combined with her artistic talent, her persistence, objectivity, and dedication were central to the creation of *Squeaky's Farm*. She worked tirelessly, donating her time and talent, happy to develop "one more" new idea or a proposed variation of an illustration while I worked on text in Walla Walla. A nine-hour time difference made our rush communications challenging, but Bron always came through, consistently professional, unbelievably focused, willing to work until she got it "right" for *Squeaky's Farm*. She masterfully juggled nurture of felines, family, and friends with my need to keep moving forward with the book. Bron rescued and cared for a sizeable number of stray cats and ferals during the time this book was in process. She has nurtured many cats into kinder, gentler lives, two of whom appear in Bron's illustrations for "The Rule" at the beginning of *Squeaky's Farm*.

Barbara Rogers Wilson is an incredibly gifted retired university professor of history and literature. If you're curious about the Dark Ages, Barbara will enchant you with her expertise. She exudes enlightenment, compassion, and joy. Even casual conversation with her is a learning experience. World traveler, animal lover, writer of novelized history, harpist, computer techie, humanitarian, pickle ball queen. One of her two dogs, Devi, is a cat wannabe. What a blessing to have met Barbara just when I needed someone with an editor's mind to help me structure the hodgepodge of my evolving manuscript. Barbara's interest in Squeaky's story jump-started me into disciplined writing mode. She skillfully and joyfully guided me on my mission to honor the tender story I held in my heart. What greater gift can you give another than to nurture their creativity?

Diane Venberg is Squeaky's rescuer and her godmother, and my good friend since Seattle days. Diane knows so much about cats and cat care, she should write a book. She's a vocal defender of animal rights and a knowledgeable, loving, reliable pet-sitter. She's active in trap/neuter/return programs for feral cats, and is an extraordinary human to her many rescued and adopted cats. I will always be grateful that she rescued Squeaky and tricked me into adopting her! Squeaky still loves the handmade wool, catnip pillow Diane sent to her in Spain, one of many thoughtful gifts mailed from Seattle to Lagar La Señora.

Scott Parker (a.k.a. Tío Roberto) is my rock, my true love, my fellow adventurer who blends science and logic with a freethinking, creative spirit. My *íntimo amigo*. Squeaky loves you as much as I do. What a Threesome we were at Lagar La Señora—Squeaky's Farm, Tio Roberto's Vineyard, and Doña Carolina's Kitchen. Thank you for always being so supportive and for your limitless encouragement of my dream to write about our lives with Squeaky in Spain.

Bobbie Mason. "Babysitting Blues" came full circle in Walla Walla when we met Bobbie Mason. Bobbie is a serious professional when it comes to caring for animals whose families are out of town. No way does Bobbie just come in the house, feed the cat, and leave. When Bobbie realized Squeaky was afraid, hiding under the bed, she sat down on the floor by the bed and read to Squeaky until Squeaky came out of hiding. Scott and I should have thought of that all those times in Spain! That's just one of the many ways Bobbie shows she loves and respects animals. Bobbie built a trust relationship with Squeaky, visit by visit, and was quick to figure out how to coax Squeaky out of her rebellious moments, to honor the impact of Squeaky's Spanish adventures on her behavior, to show respect for Squeaky's likes and dislikes, but enforce the rules of the house. And, if Squeaky is having a bad day, Bobbie understands that a new little toy or trinket always smoothes the way for a Squeaky love-in.

Scott's brother **Dick** and his wife **Sherry,** my sister **Harriet** and her husband **Bud** had to handle urgent and on-going family matters while we were adventuring in Spain. We are grateful to all four of you for facilitating the opportunity to live our dream and for your encouragement to write this book.

Dev and **Luke Traver.** Scott's dear friend and his son jetted into our Spanish world to help us clear fence lines and burn huge piles of pruned olive branches. These two hard working, tender-hearted muscle men tore through the job like a locomotive speeding through a tunnel. What fun it was to watch Dev, Luke and Scott work side by side. Squeaky sensibly didn't get under foot.

Shannon Thorne. Cheese Queen and Dancing Diva, friend and cat lover who spent several vacations with us at the farm. She spoiled Squeaky by sending her surprise packages of cat toys from Seattle and took great delight in observing Squeaky's hunting prowess in the *campo*. But Shannon's heart belonged to Mama. The two spirited curmudgeons met at Lagar La Señora and became fast friends. Shannon pampered a sick Mama with cuddles, pep talks, and all the attention she wanted. She kindly applied antibiotic ointments to Mama's eye several times a day in hopes that Mama would get well.

The new owners of Lagar La Señora, **John and Charmian**, have spent the last five years loving the farm their own way. They are devoted to the vineyard, make their own wine in the *bodega*, rev up the tractor for all those *campo* jobs, and often sit on the *era* with visiting friends to watch the stars at night. We enjoy hearing their Lagar La Señora news.

Special thanks to **Carla Perry of Dancing Moon Press** for her professional book production expertise, and to **John Wollring** for his creation of clean scans for the book.

Photos by **Henk Zweers** and **Liesbeth van Vliet** inspired the nature illustrations Bron created for *Squeaky's Farm*. If you'd like to see more nature photography, go to their website, www.Discover-Extremadura.com.

Other websites of interest:
Bron's art at www.bronwynholmes.com
Barbara's books at www.environmentalprotectionbooks.com
Diane's cat informational resources and services at
www.kittystarservices.com

Carolyn Parker

At age five, I was plopped down on a thirty-two acre farm when my family moved to Virginia. We had no indoor plumbing, minimal electricity, and a coal stove for heat. Almost fifty years later, when I saw Lagar La Señora for the first time, I was not concerned about its lack of amenities. I understood the concept of "fixer-upper."

An inspirational academic year in Spain before graduating from Mary Baldwin College created the frame around a life devoted to travel, Spanish cuisine, and artisan products. My interests in cooking, wine, olive oil, country wisdom, and writing were inspired by that academic experience.

After college, my jobs were dreams-come-true for a liberal arts major—bilingual secretary, manuscript typist, art gallery director, employment with an import company specializing in Spanish wines, and then sole owner of a small olive oil brokerage and distribution company. Along the way,

I learned to love cats and to recognize their importance in my life. All these elements entwined my love for Squeaky, Scott, and life lived simply, which led to the writing of *Squeaky's Farm*.